Family is *everything*

DARE TO *Embrace*

THE MAXWELL SERIES

S.B. ALEXANDER

Dare to Embrace

Book Seven: The Maxwell Series

Copyright © 2019 by S.B. Alexander

All rights reserved.

First Edition

Print ISBN: 978-1-7329767-9-5

Visit: www.sbalexander.com
Editor: Red Adept Editing, www.redadeptediting.com
Cover Design by Hang Le: http://www.byhangle.com

No part of this book may be reproduced in any form or by any electronic or mechanical means, including information storage and retrieval systems, without written permission from the author, except for the use of brief quotations in a book review. Please do not participate in or encourage piracy of copyrighted materials in violation of the author's rights. Thank you for respecting the hard work of the author.

This is a work of fiction. Names, characters, places and incidents either are the product of the author's imagination or are used fictitiously, and any resemblance to locales, events, business establishments, or actual persons-living or dead-is entirely coincidental.

Adult Content Warning: The content contained is the book includes adult language and sexual content. This book is intended for adult audiences 17 years of age and older.

CHAPTER 1
KADE

The aroma of roast and potatoes filled our spacious kitchen as I turned the oven down to warm. Then I lowered the recessed lighting, set the table, opened a bottle of red wine, and flicked on the stereo.

Beethoven floated out of the built-in speakers overhead, setting the mood for the night I had planned with my beautiful wife.

Once I was done, I ambled into our master bathroom and lit the candles around the Jacuzzi-style tub, which could fit two grown adults easily. I debated whether to fill the tub but decided to wait. The water wouldn't be hot, and Lacey loved to soak in the hot, soapy water.

All I needed now was Lacey. I checked my watch. She was fifteen minutes late.

Don't panic, dude. It's rush hour, and she's coming in from Portland. So that means she has to drive through Boston.

Still, I tapped on her name. I had to know where she was. The last text I'd gotten from her was when she was leaving Portland a few hours ago.

The line went directly to her voice mail.

She was probably in a bad spot with no coverage.

After I left her a message, I made my way back into the kitchen, when the doorbell rang. My mind instantly went to the dark side—something had happened to Lacey.

My pulse was erratic as I wound my way through our large first floor, passing an open high-ceiling living room before answering the door.

When I laid eyes on Maiken, my heart rate slowed, and I swallowed a growl. With Lacey due home, the last thing I wanted were distractions. We only had four days together before she had to return to Portland. My agenda was to lock us in our house, shut out the world, and make love to her nonstop. I wanted to christen every room—something we hadn't done yet because whenever she'd been home on a break during the last year, we'd had teenagers living with us, including the one standing before me.

Maiken beamed up at me like a lost puppy, his blue eyes filled with struggle and confusion. "Can I come in?"

I didn't see a suitcase, so that was good. I wasn't one to turn my back on family, but I wasn't ready to deal with more drama. I'd had enough when Maiken and his siblings, Ethan, Emma, and Marcus were living with us. I'd stepped up to lend a hand when his mom needed help while she took care of her sister, who had recently passed from breast cancer.

Four teenagers living with Lacey and me had been maddening and frustrating. Not a moment's peace. Not a moment to myself. Not a moment to make love to my wife in privacy.

I now understood what my old man had gone through when Kelton, Kross, Kody, and I had been in high school, although my brothers and I had been harder to tame than my cousins. Well, maybe not Marcus, who was quite the rebellious one out of his siblings.

I waved Maiken in, but fuck, my cousin had better have a good excuse for being at my house. I scanned the yard and driveway before I closed the door. "Where's your car?" He lived about three miles from me.

"I jogged over." He ran a hand through his sandy-blond hair. "Do you have a minute?"

I really didn't, but Lacey hadn't pulled in yet, and I could use a distraction so I didn't give myself a heart attack over worrying about my wife.

I padded into the kitchen. "A minute. Lacey is due home."

"Nice," he said. "Something smells good." He made himself comfortable on a stool at the island as though he were living here again.

"Is your mom okay?" I felt compelled to ask. His family had been plagued with bad luck since his father had passed almost two years ago.

"She's fine."

I turned off the oven. "Is it Quinn?"

He lowered his gaze to his hands.

Shit. Did they break up?

I sat down across from him. "What happened?" I remembered the day Lacey had broken up with me like it was yesterday.

"I've been a complete ass to you during this Pitt and Lorenzino mess."

"Kade?"

"No, it's my turn to talk." *If I don't, you'll be naked in the span of a minute.*

She crossed her legs and gave me her full attention.

"You said some things that day in my theater room that I've been turning over and over in my head. I know the pain from the death of a loved one. I also know how far you've come in the six months we've been together. I'm not perfect either. We'll both have nightmares and memories of our turmoil. But, Lace, I don't have PTSD. I'm learning about the symptoms and how to support you. I want to protect you from everything, including your PTSD. I know I can't. I know it's up to you to heal. I also know I need to support you and not shut you out." I exhaled. "Baby, please, never for one second believe that I think you're pathetic. I'm sorry if I made you feel that way and for everything else." *My practiced speech came out easily.*

She folded the corners of the pages of her chemistry book. Her eyes were downcast. A brittle silence dangled.

Say something. Anything. *The quietness drove the nausea to churn inside my stomach.*

"It's..." Her voice broke. "This is hard for me." She kept her eyes on her book.

My pulse went into overdrive. I'd so fucked up. My heart skipped several beats. I couldn't lose this girl.

She lifted her soft green eyes, worrying her bottom lip. "I have so much going on that I don't know how to process it all. I could be in danger. I have a new family, albeit a mob family. I have baseball. I want that baseball scholarship to ASU. I have an illness that stops me in my tracks and causes others to freak out along with me. I don't want anyone's pity or sympathy. The only way I can do that is to tackle a couple of things at a time." *She pushed out all the air in her lungs as her cheeks puffed.*

Please don't say it. Please don't say it. *I was squeezing the energy out of every one of my muscles.*

"But..." She held my gaze. "I know you're sorry. I know you love me. But until my other problems are behind me, I can't work on a relationship. I just can't."

"So that's it? You're breaking up with me?"

Her shoulder came up to her ear. "I guess. I guess I am."

Maiken snapped his fingers, shattering the memory of when I'd walked into Lacey's bedroom seven years ago. "You checked out, man."

I blinked. "Sorry. What were you saying?"

He picked at the skin on one of his fingers. "Sex."

My eyes widened. "You two broke up because of sex?" I didn't mean to sound surprised.

He lifted his head quickly. "Oh no. We didn't break up."

I relaxed my features. Quinn was a great girl, and she was good for Maiken. He seemed happy with her in his life.

So he wanted to talk sex. Since his father had passed, I'd become his mentor of sorts, which I enjoyed unless I was bailing him or any of his siblings out of the principal's office at Kensington High.

"I'm listening." I wasn't sure I could give him much advice on the topic other than to make sure he practiced safe sex.

"I think Quinn and I are ready, but what if I don't please her? What if it's not what I thought sex would be? Or if afterwards, she doesn't want anything to do with me?"

I rubbed my chin, dipping back to my first time having sex with a girl in the tenth grade. We'd both wanted to get our first time out of the way. We hadn't been in love either. I couldn't recall, though, if I'd been expecting much. Actually, I'd been too nervous to think that night. Afterward, the girl and I had laughed at how weird the experience had been.

"Did you feel apprehensive with Lacey?" Maiken asked. "I don't want details, just..." His attention was fixated on me like I had all the answers.

I studied his desperate plea for advice. I never thought I would be giving anyone pointers on sex, at least not until Lacey and I had our own kids. Even then I wasn't sure what I would tell my son or daughter. Although if we had girls, I would kill the fucker who dared to put his hands on my baby girl.

Maiken tapped on the island counter. "Man, it looks like you've seen a ghost. It's okay. We don't have to talk about sex."

Blinking, I chuckled. "It's cool. My first time with a chick was awkward. I'm not going to lie. But I wasn't in love with her."

"You mean Lacey wasn't your first?" Horror etched his tone.

"No, and I wasn't her first either. But we didn't meet until our senior year. Look, Maiken, I suggest you and Quinn talk about your feelings before you have sex. Make sure you're both ready. And above all else, practice safe sex. You and her have a future to think about with college."

"Do you think she's on the pill?" he asked, sounding like his question was directed at himself rather than me. "Don't answer that. I'm so nervous. But it's getting to the point that anytime I'm around her, I want to..."

"I get it," I said. "Believe me, when you're in love with someone, that feeling of wanting to lock yourself in a room with her is always there." *Like now.* I checked the time again.

Where the fuck was Lacey?

Suddenly, pain gripped my temples, and I winced.

What the fuck? I hadn't had a migraine since my tumor was removed three years ago.

Tumor? No fucking way. The surgeon had removed all of the benign mass, but he'd also said it was possible another mass could grow back. I'd had scans done every year since. *No, you haven't, dude. It's been over a year since your last one.*

"Kade, you're seeing a ghost again," Maiken drawled in a lazy Southern accent, which I hadn't heard from him in a while. "Are you okay?"

My vision blurred for a split second as my gaze rounded on him. "Just the onset of a headache."

I blew out a breath when I heard the front door open. Then Lacey's voice peppered the air. I took in another breath, more to help the knot in my stomach unwind at the fact that she was home.

I plastered on a smile, albeit a fake one since the pain in my head was throbbing.

Lacey glided in, dressed in shorts, showing off her toned legs. A tight T-shirt accentuated her beautiful breasts, and her long, wavy brown hair was piled up on her head. But what had my dick throbbing were those green eyes of hers that had a way of sucking me in each and every time.

She swung her gaze from Maiken to me. "What's wrong?"

Maiken rose. "I was asking Kade for some advice. But then his head started hurting."

Lacey rushed over to me. "Headache? Like a migraine?" Her voice faltered.

Fuck. I knew what she was thinking.

I pulled her to me and kissed her on the lips. "It's nothing."

5

"I'm out of here," Maiken said. "I'll let myself out." His shoes squeaked on the floor as he left.

Once I heard the door click, I buried my hands in Lacey's thick hair. "Hi."

She cupped my face, her chest rising and falling as she studied me. "When was the last time you had a headache?"

I chuckled. "Seriously, it's nothing to worry about."

"You said that last time, and it turned out to be a tumor," she complained. "It's been a while since you had a checkup."

I hadn't had a moment to myself with teenagers in my life. "I know. And I'll make an appointment with the doc."

She sighed as she threw her arms around me. "Sorry I'm late. Traffic was brutal."

I shaped her hips before my hands landed on her ass. "Did you get my voice mail?"

"I did. I should've called, but I was set on getting home." Her tongue darted out.

My dick jumped. "I made a roast."

She flattened her hands on my chest. "Maybe later." Then her hands were expertly and slowly dancing down my abs until she was unbuckling my belt. "I'm all yours for four days."

Suddenly, that throbbing pain in my head settled in my groin. I scooped her up and into my arms then carried her into our bedroom. No amount of pain was going to ruin our evening.

Once in our bedroom, I set her down on our king bed. "I'll start the bath water. Be right back." I hurried into the en suite bathroom, turned on the hot water, poured in a copious amount of bubble bath soap, and added some eucalyptus crystals she loved.

On the way back into the bedroom, I began stripping, but when I laid eyes on her, I came to an abrupt halt.

She was propped up on a pillow, naked, legs open, massaging her breasts.

Fuuuuck!

I wasn't a pubescent teenager, but suddenly I felt like I was about to lose my load. It had been too fucking long since I'd seen Lacey naked. It had been a lifetime since I'd seen her tweaking her nipples or licked that sweet-tasting pussy of hers.

"You gonna stare or do something about Mr. Steel?" She pointed at my dick straining to get out of my boxer briefs.

I shucked the rest of my clothes, and when my cock sprang free, her green eyes went wide, drowning me in love and lust.

She crooked her finger. "I want to taste Mr. Steel first."

My dick was steel, all right.

I dug my bare feet into the plush carpet as I closed the distance between us. By the time I reached the bed, she'd scooted to the edge and tugged my underwear down, and before I could say anything, her mouth was around my dick.

I growled, loud and deep, as my eyes rolled back in my head. Then I burrowed my fingers into her hair as her hands wrapped around my shaft.

Holy fuck!

I wasn't going to last a damn second.

She sucked hard as she played with my balls.

Reality started to fade when I remembered the water. "The bath." My voice was weak at best.

She giggled.

I lifted her in my arms. "Let's continue this in the bathtub."

CHAPTER 2
LACEY

I yawned as I stretched, blinking awake to the sunlight streaking in through the slats in the shutters that weren't closed all the way.

I nestled into the soft cotton sheets, watching Kade. The man looked peaceful as he slept with one hand under the pillow and the other tucked close to his chest.

It had been too long since I woke up with him next to me. Too long since I could reach out and touch his rugged jaw or broad chest or toned biceps or even have my way with him.

He didn't travel with me during baseball season. When I'd first signed my contract, I had wanted Kade to join me at every game, and in the beginning, he had on occasion. But when we broke ground on our new house and he'd become the guardian of four of his teenage cousins, his time wasn't his own anymore. Plus, he had his job as a manager of one of my dad's nightclubs.

Despite his responsibilities, I wasn't complaining. Kade wasn't a traveler. I'd known that going into my contract and our marriage. He wasn't the type to sit around in the stadium night after night. He loved me with all his heart, and I loved him beyond what I could put into words. His happiness was precious to me. So I was cool with living in a rented apartment in Portland, Maine, during the baseball season.

I wasn't that far from home, so if I had a day off, I could zip down to spend it with Kade and the family.

Still, lying next to him was rare during the season. Sadly, I hadn't gotten picked for the All-Star team, but on the flip side, I had four days to spend with Kade.

I sighed as I thought about the night before. I had messed up. I'd wanted nothing more than to make love to him, but as soon as he set me in the bathtub, I hadn't been able to keep my eyes open. Between the hot water and his strong arms, I'd felt more relaxed than I had in quite some time.

Baseball season drained the energy out of me. I loved every second of playing ball. I got high from the energy on the field and in the dugouts. I loved the fans, the adrenaline rush, the wins, the celebrations, everything about my career. I was living my dream, which I'd had reservations about before the Portland Sea Dogs signed me. I was a female who had finally broken through a barrier into a male-dominated arena, and the road leading up to the Sea Dogs had been a challenging one.

But playing ball had its downsides—the travel, living out of a suitcase, and the sleepless nights without Kade at my side led to loneliness. At times, jealousy reared its ugly head at how my teammates could go home to their spouses or significant others after a game or, on most nights, when we played at home.

I gnawed on my bottom lip as my gaze drifted from Kade to our private hideaway. I barely knew my own bedroom. Lying there felt odd, like I didn't even live there. Maybe that was because the light-blue walls were in need of pictures or artwork. The large space could certainly use a comfy chair or two near our French doors, which led out to a stone-stamped patio.

I continued to chew on my lip, letting my mind wander about decorating ideas until my gaze landed on a signed baseball that was encased on my dresser. Suddenly, the conversation with my agent, Tara, was front and center.

She'd been one of the reasons I was late getting home. I'd pulled over for about fifteen minutes to talk to her. She'd called to inform me that a Triple-A ball club was interested in me. My jaw had dropped to my lap when she'd said those words. Since I was a little girl, I'd always dreamed of playing major-league baseball, and Triple-A was the next step in that climb to the top.

"You're deep in thought." Kade's voice was husky and raspy, and *oh my*. Goose bumps fired along my arms. He reached over and flattened one of his calloused hands on my abs. "Care to share?" His sleepy copper eyes were sexy as he grinned, showing those dimples that sent erotic heat to settle in between my legs.

Baseball and any offers could wait.

I snuggled closer to his hot bod, literally and figuratively. Winters were the best when I could curl up next to him and steal the warmth of his body. But I wasn't cold in the least at the moment. "I'm sorry about last night."

He moved my hair off my face. "I know you were tired."

I slipped my leg in between his, relishing the feel of his muscled thighs. "How's your head?" My heart had fallen out of my chest when Maiken said my husband had a headache.

"It's fine. But I do have pain elsewhere." He waggled his eyebrows, his eyes shimmering in the morning light.

Butterflies took flight in my stomach.

He dragged a hand down from my face to my breasts and began tracing a circle around my nipple. The act was soothing and erotic, and I moaned in delight.

Before I could take my next breath, Kade was on top of me with his hands on either side of my head, his erection grazing my inner thigh.

My legs had a mind of their own, falling open and giving him full access to do as he pleased.

He groaned as he licked his way down my neck, stopping to give my breasts equal attention.

I didn't want his mouth on my nipples. The pulsating need in between my legs demanded his tongue, begging for him to take what I hadn't had in months. So I wiggled my body upward, praying, hoping he would get the hint.

He chuckled. The man was torturing, teasing, and taking his sweet-ass time as my clit throbbed endlessly.

"I need you, Kade. Now!" My voice cracked on each word as I sucked in air.

He gave me one of his sexy grins as he lingered on my belly button. "I want you to spell it out, baby." His tone was playful. "Give me details."

Ass. He was throwing my words in my face. I always wanted details of what he would do to me. Dirty talk and foreplay were something I craved, but at that very moment, I wanted action.

"I want you to lick me." I shimmied higher on the bed, hoping I could meet him halfway.

He laughed again.

"Payback is hell, Kade Maxwell." I hoped to scare him a little. But who was I kidding? My husband didn't scare so easily.

Lazily, he dragged his tongue down to the apex of my legs and kissed everywhere but the one spot I wanted him to touch.

I growled low and was about to take matters in my own hands when he sat on his heels, stroking his rock-hard erection. His copper eyes gleamed as his eyelids became hooded. What a sight I had before me. I was no longer desperate to get myself off. I was desperate to watch him. I was desperate to please him.

His chest rose and fell as he licked his lips. "Play with yourself."

How many times had we done this very thing over FaceTime? Phone sex was the best and the only way to sate the hunger we had for each other when I was away.

I wasn't one to argue, not when pleasure was involved.

I planted my feet on the mattress and pointed my knees at the ceiling. My hand slid down my stomach slowly. My eyes were peeled to the godlike man before me.

"Circle your clit." His demand sent an electric current straight to my clit.

My hand rushed to do as he commanded.

The minute my fingers touched my throbbing nub, I shot off the bed. "I'm not going to last."

He grabbed my wrist, captured my finger in his mouth, and sucked—a move that I was sure was meant to distract him and me from sending us both over the edge.

His gaze was glued to mine as he continued to swirl his tongue around my finger.

Whatever motive he had for holding my finger hostage, I didn't care. What I cared about was having him inside of me.

So I sat up and gripped his erection with my free hand.

He let out a low rumble as he traded my finger for my lips. His tongue dove in hard and fast, devouring me.

My skin hummed. My breath was labored. My mind was mush.

He groaned and moaned as I continued to stroke what was mine. I loved how he reacted to my touch even after seven years together. The spark that had ignited between us that first day I'd pulled a gun on him in the high school parking lot was brighter than ever.

I matched his kiss, sucking on his tongue as a tingling sensation spread throughout my body. "I need you now, baby."

He pushed me back, and before I could take a breath, he thrust inside me hard.

I whimpered.

The word "fuck" dropped from his lips. He stilled as he flashed those heavy-lidded eyes. "Wrap your legs around me," he said in a husky tone.

Once we were in his favorite position, he began pumping, slowly at first. "Play with your nipples."

I shook my head. "I need you to bite them, hard."

He cocked any eyebrow, obliging.

I squealed, my eyes rolling back in my head. Then the next thing I knew, he was flipping me over until I was on all fours and he was shoving his steel erection into me from behind.

I tossed a look over my shoulder, holding my bottom lip hostage.

His eyes were wild, crazed, full of lust and love and so much more. His chest expanded, and his biceps bunched as he held on to my hips. He looked like a god—all man, all muscle, all mine.

He hesitated for a moment as though he were trying to gain control of whatever was going on in his head. Then he went from zero to fifty in a matter of seconds, rocking, thrusting, and pumping. Without warning, he flipped me on my back.

I once again wrapped my legs around him as we fell into a rhythm, both of us bucking and rocking. Each thrust became faster, harder, hotter, and higher as he took me to the edge.

Then he pulled out.

I shot up. "What's wrong?" I barely spoke the words.

He buried his head between my legs, latched on to my clit, and sucked.

Oh, crap on a cracker.

In two seconds, I was screaming his name, arching my back, and clutching the sheets. I dove off the cliff into pure bliss as bright stars flashed behind my eyelids.

My toes curled as he shoved inside me, pumping and grunting. "I love the crap out of you, Lacey Maxwell." Then he stilled, his eyelids drifting shut briefly as he rode out his orgasm, pulsating inside me. Sweat dripped down his temples as he rubbed his hand down my chest and stomach. "I can't believe I lasted that long."

I wasn't surprised. Stamina was his middle name. The man could go forever, sometimes pleasing me two or three times before he orgasmed.

He rolled off me and propped his head in his hand as he lay on his side, facing me. "Give me five minutes, and we'll go again."

I laughed, trying to regulate my breathing. "I think I need food first." I started to get up.

He swung his arm over me, caging me down. "You're not going anywhere. We're just getting started."

My stomach growled.

He arched his eyebrow, grinning. "We do need to christen the kitchen."

Giggling, I kissed him. "That island is big enough."

He traced lazy circles around my nipple. "The island, the dining table, the couch, the deck, the patio."

My gaze fell to Mr. Steel growing as Kade rattled off all the places he wanted to make love. I couldn't help but play with myself. I clutched his dick and began stroking his velvety shaft as goose bumps blanketed my body.

He shuddered a breath. "I've missed you so fucking much." His tone was a mixture of love and sadness.

Our marriage was as solid as a slab of granite. Nothing could come between Kade and me. But in that moment, a knot of guilt settled in my stomach. It was my fault that he was sad. It was my fault I was never home. It was my fault that I wanted baseball as much as I wanted him.

Groaning, he rolled his hips as I stroked him hard. Any guilt I had waned for the moment. In its place, the need to see him come apart was all I cared about. I crawled down and captured his large dick in my mouth.

He moaned loudly as his fingers dove into my hair.

I swirled my tongue around the tip, teasing and licking before taking him deep.

When I did, he bucked off the bed, grasping on to my hair. "I love it when you suck me off." His voice cracked on another loud moan.

Just hearing him made me want to orgasm right then and there. But at the moment, pleasing him was my number-one priority.

I sucked, licked, stroked, and took him as deep as my gag reflex would allow.

He spewed loud grunts, growls, and groans, heightening my senses and making my pussy throb to the point that I didn't need anything to get me off except seeing him come apart.

His leg muscles began to tense, and his hands tightened in my hair. "Suck harder." His breathing ramped up.

With all the energy I had, I gripped his balls and sucked him until he was groaning his release. He barely let me swallow before I was on my back. His tongue stroked my clit once then twice, and when he shoved two fingers inside me, I screamed his name, my body shuddering through my release.

He lingered, kissing my inner thighs, smiling as I tried to regulate my breathing. I rode out the longest and best orgasm in quite some time.

He crawled up my body then pecked me on the lips. "Good morning."

"Can we eat now?"

He chuckled. "Maybe."

I playfully swatted at him. "I need fuel to go another round."

He climbed off the bed then extended his hand. "Let's take a shower. Then we'll eat. Then round three."

Giggling, I stood up on shaky legs. After my time off, I was afraid I wouldn't be able to walk out of the house, let alone play baseball.

CHAPTER 3
KADE

Lacey ambled into the kitchen with her hair piled up on her head, her green eyes beaming, and looking as relaxed as ever.

I grinned as my dick jerked in my jeans.

She lifted up on her toes and kissed me on the cheek. "Something smells wonderful."

Setting the tongs down on the counter, I gripped her chin before my lips brushed hers. "Yeah, baby. You." Her shampoo smelled like oranges and cream.

She stole a piece of bacon from the plate near the stove, her stomach growling.

"Sit your beautiful body down and let me wait on you."

Her hand clutched my groin. "Aren't we christening the kitchen?" She tugged her bottom lip between her teeth.

My eyes were ready to roll back into my head if she kept squeezing Mr. Steel. "Eat first." My voice was strained as my gaze lowered to her nipples, which were poking out of her Dodgers T-shirt. "You need fuel if I'm going to chase you around the house."

The thought of playing hide-and-seek caused my pulse to ramp up several notches. It was a game we both loved to play.

She chewed on the bacon, still holding my dick. "Hide-and-seek?" Her eyes went wide.

I kissed her on the nose as I pinched her nipple. "You know I always find you."

"Pffft. I let you," she said, sashaying over to the island.

I chuckled. "We'll see." I resumed cooking, cracking the eggs into a bowl.

"I think we should decorate our bedroom while I'm home," Lacey said. "Don't we have some pictures stored in the basement?"

I beat the eggs. "I think so." I really didn't want to do anything house related. We only had four days, and I wanted her in my arms the entire time.

A phone rang.

I tensed as I tossed a look over my shoulder. Mine was off and in the bedroom.

Her hands disappeared under the counter for a second. When they surfaced, she was tapping on the screen, and her features were pinched. "I'll be right back." She hopped off the stool and breezed out of the kitchen before I could question who the fuck was calling at seven in the morning. Or calling at all for that matter.

She was on break from baseball, so it couldn't be her manager. Maybe someone in my family was hurt and couldn't get ahold of me. I dismissed that idea. Mom and Dad lived a stone's throw across the lake. If something had happened, Dad would've been at my door if he couldn't get me on the phone.

I could barely hear Lacey as I busied myself with scrambling the eggs. My hands stopped over the pan when I heard her say "Tara."

What the fuck does she want? She only called Lacey when she had an opportunity for her or wanted to talk contracts. But her current contract with the Portland Sea Dogs wasn't up until the following year. My mind spun, remembering a conversation Lacey and I had had before she signed with the Sea Dogs.

"Are you sure you're okay with me on the road all the time?" she'd asked.

Hell no. I didn't want her away from me for one fucking second. When she'd gone off to college and I'd stayed behind, those four years had been brutal on me. But I couldn't deny her something she'd lived and trained for her entire life, and I wouldn't.

"I want you to live your dream, but I do want kids in the near future," I'd replied.

She'd beamed up at me. "We'll start our family when my contract with the Sea Dogs is up. I promise."

It had been pointless to discuss what-ifs. What if she extended her contract? What if she signed with another team? What if she decided she didn't want kids until she retired? All those questions had plagued me then and every now and again during the last two years.

Lacey waltzed back in and over to her stool. Her gaze was glued to her phone.

I carried the bowl of scrambled eggs to the island. "What did Tara want?"

Her head shot up. "You heard?" Panic laced her tone.

I gripped the edge of the marble top. "I heard you say Tara."

She slumped her shoulders as though she were relieved that I'd only heard Tara's name and not their conversation.

I cocked my head, wondering why the fuck she was so panicked. "Well?"

She shrugged, gnawing on her lip. "It's nothing."

I let out a chuckle that wasn't light or funny. "And you're lying. Tara is your agent, which means she's calling you because she has an opportunity for you."

The doorbell rang.

Neither of us moved as we stared at one another.

I lifted my eyebrows, prodding Lacey to answer me or say something. But she sat there, seemingly perplexed as though she didn't know what to say.

The bell rang again.

Cursing under my breath, I left Lacey to answer the door. Whoever was standing on the porch had better have a damn good reason for disturbing us at an early hour. I wasn't in the mood for anyone else's problems.

Blowing out a breath, I opened the door.

Christine Maxwell stood on the porch, appearing frantic and teary-eyed.

"What did Marcus do now?" I asked, assuming her crying had something to do with her teenage son even though she had seven other kids besides Marcus.

She flicked strands of her ash-blond hair off her forehead. "Is Marcus here, by chance? I tried to call you."

Maybe shutting off my phone wasn't such a good idea if people were going to show up on my doorstep instead.

I waved her in. "I haven't seen Marcus since the cookout at my parents' house last week."

I let out a frustrated sigh. The kid wasn't even my son. He wasn't living with me anymore either. Yet he still had a way of driving me insane. Given how rebellious he was, I wouldn't be surprised if he was passed out drunk somewhere. He'd started drinking when he was living with me, but I thought he was on the straight and narrow since his mom had returned from Georgia and bought a house for the family.

Christine folded her arms across her chest as she climbed over the threshold and into the foyer. "His bed hasn't been slept in. Maiken and Ethan are out looking. Jasper doesn't know anything. Marcus's girlfriend, Sloane, hasn't seen him either."

Lacey's footsteps echoed as her bare feet slapped on the wood floor. "What's going on?"

"I can't find Marcus," Christine said, on the verge of tears. "He's been out of control lately, angry at the world. I'm afraid he's drinking again."

I shoved my fingers through my hair, hating that I was right about the drinking. My brothers and I hadn't turned to liquor when our sister had died. But we had gotten into one too many fights, to the point that Kody had ended up in a coma.

Lacey hugged Christine. "I'm so sorry. Have you checked with the Ashford police?"

Christine nodded. "They don't have any record of him, and it's too soon to file a missing person's report." She broke down in tears. "I just don't know how to help him. He stopped seeing his psychiatrist."

Fuck. The morning had started off with mind-blowing sex, but as the minutes ticked by, the day was going to shit.

"Kade will help look for Marcus," Lacey said, giving me her puppy-dog look. "Right, honey?" Her tone could melt butter.

What was I saying? Her tone was melting me in every possible way.

"Of course," I said, gritting my teeth as I silently shouted cuss words in my head.

She ushered Christine into the kitchen.

And just like that, I was back to wrangling in a teenager if I could find him.

"Lacey, can we talk a second?" I asked.

She backtracked while Christine went ahead of her.

When we were alone, Lacey planted her hands on my chest. "We can talk later. Right now, go find Marcus."

A growl barreled out of my chest. How the hell would I find the boy? The cops didn't have any record of him.

CHAPTER 4
KADE

Ten minutes later, I was in my truck on my way to Sloane's house. I figured I would start there. Christine had checked with Sloane, but my gut was telling me the girl was covering for Marcus. I didn't know her that well, but she and Marcus had been tied at the hip since she'd shown up at the beginning of his freshman year, which was about ten months ago.

As I turned out of my driveway, my phone rang. Kody's name flashed across the dashboard.

"Bro, you better get down to the club."

I laughed, mainly out of frustration. If anyone knew not to bother me during Lacey's time at home, it was Kody. So something major must have happened. "Did someone break in?"

"Um... You could say that."

I rolled my window down to let in fresh morning air, even though humidity was thick. "Did you call the cops?"

Kody hissed out a breath. "I don't think we should. But you may want to call Christine."

I stopped at the crossroads outside the Maxwell estate, shaking my head at no one. "Marcus?"

"How did you know?"

"I'll tell you when I get there." I ended the call then banged on the steering wheel.

The boy was probably going to be the death of me.

I pressed on the gas a little too hard, as I turned left toward Ashford. Within fifteen minutes, I was walking into The Cave and to a scene that had my stomach in knots and my hands balled into fists at my sides.

Kody led me over to the stage, pointing at a sight that would make Christine croak.

Marcus was passed out with not one, not two, but three bottles of hard liquor next to him.

Kody set his blue gaze on me. "I didn't want to wake him."

Fuck that.

My feet pounded a little too hard on the wood floor before climbing up on stage. I was surprised the boy hadn't drowned in his own puke because his gray T-shirt was soaked in it.

I squatted down and slapped him on the face, not hard, but enough to jar him awake. "Marcus."

The boy didn't move. The only saving grace was that I could see his chest moving.

I tapped his face a bit harder. "Man, wake up."

Groaning, he swatted at me. "Go away."

I slid the bottles of liquor out of the way. "Kody, can you get some water?"

"I have something better than that," Kody said as he walked away.

"Marcus, get your ass up," I commanded in a tone that was scary even to me.

He groaned.

I seriously needed to rethink my position on kids and a big family. If Marcus's rebellious nature was any indication of what I had in store, then maybe Lacey should play ball until she was forty.

My heart went out to Christine even though I wasn't in the mood to deal with Marcus. The woman was a young widow with eight kids, and five of them were teenagers. *Whoa!*

Kody returned with a bucket in his hand.

I popped to my feet to get out of the way of what was about to happen.

Kody stood over Marcus and emptied the bucket of crushed ice on top of him.

Like lightning, Marcus sat straight up. His blue eyes were wide. His mouth was hanging open, and he was seething with a look that could kill Kody in an instant.

I crossed my arms over my chest. "Get your ass up," I commanded harshly.

He threw me the middle finger as his eyes surveyed me then Kody. "Fuck off."

Kody went to grab Marcus by the collar, but I held up my hand.

"Kody, can you call the cops and let them know we've had a break-in?"

Tough love was how my old man had taught us. When the triplets had gotten out of hand, especially when Kross and Kody had retaliated against one of our enemies in high school, he'd sent the triplets off to a private school.

Kody whipped out his cell phone, his blue eyes dancing with pleasure.

Marcus, on the other hand, glared daggers at me.

Bending over, I got in his face. "Don't fuck with me. I'm in a bad mood this morning."

"Yeah," Kody said into his phone. "I would like to report a break-in."

Marcus shot to his feet, stumbling as he tried to get the phone out of Kody's hand. Kody was quicker, moving away as he bobbed his head at whoever was on the other end of the line.

"Please don't call the cops," Marcus whined, losing that bad-boy attitude.

I gripped his arm and practically dragged him off the stage and to a chair. "Sit."

He did as he was told. "You can't call the cops," he pleaded.

"Maybe a jail cell would do you some good." I didn't believe it would, but scaring him straight might work, just like it had when Sloane had hit his brother Maiken with her car. After that had happened, Marcus was a new person.

I dragged a chair next to him and nodded at Kody.

He lowered his phone and strutted over to the bar. "Let me know if you need me to redial."

Marcus shot to his feet. "No!"

"Sit down," I said in a harsh tone.

The day was becoming a clusterfuck. I wanted to pummel the kid. I had a lot of patience, but I was at the end of my rope. He'd given me a lot of lip when he lived with me, but I'd always bitten my tongue, hoping that it was just a short phase of depression over the death of his dad.

I shoved my hands through my hair. "What happened to you? Why are you drinking again? And you're going to work off the liquor you drank."

Marcus winced as though I were screaming at him. "Life happened."

I pulled out my phone and called Lacey.

"Are you seriously calling the cops?" His tone dripped with fear.

He should be frightened.

I lifted a shoulder. "Maybe."

Kody returned with a glass of tomato juice. "Drink this."

Marcus grabbed the glass and downed the juice.

Lacey answered. "Did you find him?"

"He's at The Cave," I said. "Let Christine know I'll drop him at her house."

"Okay," Lacey said before she hung up.

I pocketed my phone. "Your mom is worried out of her mind."

His body slumped in the chair as he pulled on strands of his brown hair. Then he started crying. "I don't want her to see me like this."

I briefly closed my eyes, wishing I could restart the day or go back two hours when I was making love to my wife, not once, but twice. The kid needed serious help, and as much as I could talk to him and give him advice, I didn't think anything I said would resonate with him. Nevertheless, I said in a soft voice, "Talk to me, Marcus." As moody as I was and as mad as I was with him, my heart broke for what he was going through.

I didn't think this drunken escapade had anything to do with the death of his father.

He wiped his eyes with his fingers. "Sloane broke up with me."

Silence filled the club except for Kody mulling around behind the bar.

I sighed as I rested my elbows on my knees. "That sucks. Did she give you a reason?"

"She's moving. Something about long-distance relationships don't work. Why does everyone leave me?"

Man, I couldn't answer that. But I could feel his pain as if I were reliving the day the paramedics had wheeled Karen's dead body out of our garage. I'd felt angry, sad, empty, and lost, like I'd fallen down a black hole into nothing, and the pain had only intensified.

"Drinking isn't the way to cope," I said. "I might have an idea."

I found Kross's name in my contacts and tapped on the number.

A muscle jumped along Marcus's jaw. "Seriously, are you calling the cops?"

Standing, I flicked my head toward the back of the club. "Go get yourself cleaned up. There's a bathroom in my office."

Marcus hesitated until I said, "Hey, bro," into the phone. Then he was on his feet, walking away.

"What's up?" Kross asked. "Everything okay?"

"Peachy."

"Oh no. Did Lacey not come home?" he asked.

"She did. But I need your help. Can you head home and spend some time with Marcus in the boxing ring? I think showing him some moves might help him channel his aggression a little." Kross was still boxing professionally, but he was also teaching at a gym in Boston.

"I can this weekend," he said. "What did he do now?"

I chuckled. "What doesn't Marcus do?" I asked the question more to myself.

"Good point. Hey, man, I was going to call you. I heard something last night and wasn't sure if it was true. Is Lacey moving up into Triple-A?"

I twitched. "What?" My brain suddenly felt like someone had slapped it from one side of my skull to the other. "Where did you hear that?" So that was the reason Tara had called.

"A couple of players from the Pawtucket Sox were in the gym last night. I overheard them dropping Lacey's name around about Triple-A. They left before I could ask them any questions."

Fuck me.

"I got to run." I had a wife to corner.

CHAPTER 5
LACEY

I was sitting at a table in the back corner of the cafeteria at the local hospital, waiting for Becca. I hadn't seen my best friend in, like, forever. She was a nurse in the Neonatal Intensive Care Unit, or NICU as it was called.

After Kade texted me that he would be a couple of hours with Marcus, I had some time to catch up with my BFF.

I texted Becca: *I'm here.*

A young boy about five with brown curls and bright blue eyes ran up to a table near me and climbed onto a chair. As the boy smiled at me, I couldn't help but think of what my kids would look like. Would they have brown hair and green eyes like me or resemble Kade with his to-die-for copper eyes?

The boy's dad rushed up behind him with a tray of food. "Wyatt, that table is dirty. Let's sit at this one." The man, who appeared tired and had dark circles marring his brown eyes, set the food down on a clean table in front of me.

Wyatt bounced over to his dad. "I want ketchup."

The dad transferred the food from the tray to the table then proceeded to open a ketchup packet for his son.

I watched him dote on the boy and wondered why the man was in the hospital in the first place. *Did something happen to his wife? Was she in an accident? Or maybe she was having a baby.*

The latter thought made me shiver slightly as I remembered the hardness to Kade's tone when he'd said, "Tara is your agent, which means she's calling you because she has an opportunity for you." I knew what he was thinking—kids.

I'd promised him when my contract was up that we would start our family. Granted, I still had one year left before any notion of getting pregnant was practical. But I'd never thought that a Triple-A team would come knocking.

It wasn't because of my performance. I was a great pitcher. It was the industry and being a female in an all-male arena. Prior to signing me with the Sea Dogs, Tara had worked her tail off to find a team interested in me. Most of the organizations she'd spoken with had been leery of signing a female. So when the Sea Dogs bit, I had jumped on the opportunity.

Regardless, I didn't want to spend the short amount of time during this break arguing with Kade over contracts, careers, and kids. But it was inevitable.

Dread sat heavy in my stomach at the thought of how the conversation between Kade and me would play out. Yet excitement wiggled its way in. The Iowa Cubs had sent Tara an email that morning, asking when she would be able to discuss me. After our conversation the night before, Tara hadn't expected to hear from them until well after the All-Star break.

Things were happening too fast. I needed to talk to Kade before she made any deals, though.

Someone tapped on the table before the sound of a chair dragging along the floor resonated.

I blinked to find my BFF with her head angled and worry in her dark eyes. "Are you okay?"

I popped up and threw my arms around Becca. "You look fantastic." She was dressed in pink scrubs. Her dark hair was styled in one of those French pull-through braids that I'd seen on a waitress recently. Her makeup was flawless, and her nose ring glinted in the lights of the cafeteria. She seemed to be in her element working at the hospital.

She squeezed me hard. "I miss you."

We embraced for a long second, then I eased away. "When did you get the piercing?" I pointed at her nose.

Smiling, she swept her gaze over me. "A couple of months ago. Talk about looking great. I wish I was as toned as you." She gripped my biceps. "Work out much?" She snickered.

I rolled my eyes, returning to my seat. "All part of the game."

She sat in the chair opposite me. "Please tell me that you and Kade are all right."

I reared back. "What makes you think we're not?" I shouldn't have been surprised she could sense something was up since she was my best friend.

She twirled her finger around my eyes. "Girl, I see it. Something is bugging you. And as much as I love you and want to see you, you should be home with that sexy husband of yours."

"He's dealing with Marcus at the moment. And can't I see my best friend?"

She laced her fingers together on the table. "Tell me what's going on. Wait. Let me guess." She licked her red lips, studying me. "You have a glow about you. So your marriage is fine, which I guess means you had monkey sex this morning."

I glanced around the cafeteria, hoping no one had heard her, especially the little boy behind Becca. Nevertheless, I blushed hard, only because someone had to be listening. Sure enough, I locked eyes with an older couple two tables over who were looking at us.

Leaning over the table, I said, "Just let the entire room know."

She laughed loudly. "Do you know what goes on in this hospital?" She waggled her eyebrows.

I held up my hand. "Don't want to know."

"So if you and Kade are fine, then what is it? Unless you're pregnant." She sat back in her chair. "That's the only thing that could make you freak out because of your career."

I took in a breath. "If I am, I might have to sue the IUD company." I'd switched from the pill to an IUD over a year ago and only because the bloating and occasional nausea had become too much.

She leaned in. "IUDs are not one hundred percent preventive. You know that, right?"

I wasn't naive to that tidbit. "I'm not pregnant."

"Then what?"

I felt selfish that the little time we had would be spent with her listening to my problems.

That's what friends are for.

Still, I wanted to hear all about her job, her sex life, and all those things friends shared with one another.

"Let's talk about you," I said.

She reached over and grabbed my hand. "Dish about what's on your mind. We can talk about me over a drink before you leave. Right now, I'm here for you."

I swallowed thickly as Wyatt complained that he didn't have enough ketchup on his hot dog.

"A Triple-A team is interested in me."

Her lips parted. "Shut up! That's fantastic." She angled her head. "Kade doesn't know. And let me guess—he's not going to be happy."

I bobbed my head. She knew how bad Kade wanted kids and that he wanted them now.

"We agreed to get pregnant when my contract was up next year. If talks go well, though, then I could be playing for another five years." I twirled strands of my long hair around my fingers, a nervous habit of mine. "I want baseball and kids, but I don't think I can have both, or at least do both. Teams will shy away from me if they know I want to take a year off and start a family. And if I do take a year off, my gut is telling me I won't get back into baseball. Not because of me, but because teams aren't going to take a brand-new mom or one that could be having kids for the next few years. And Kade wants a baseball team full of them."

She captured a nail in between her lips. "I'm all for you breaking barriers into a man's sport."

"But?" I asked.

She leaned in. "You're not getting younger, Lacey. The sooner you start your family, the faster you can return to baseball while you're still young."

A nervous laugh escaped my lips. "But how can I get pregnant if I sign up for another five years?" It wasn't a question for her to answer. "It's not like I can play with a big belly in the way. And no organization would even consider me if I'm thinking of getting pregnant."

Her nose scrunched. "Girl, we're living in a new age. Why wouldn't a team consider you? If they don't, then they're discriminating."

In any other type of job outside of an all-male sport, I would agree with her. "Baseball isn't like a regular job that I can return to and expect to pick up where I left off. Teams don't work like that. They plan their rosters. Sure, I could go on the disabled list. But would they let me return?"

"Then you need to decide what is most important to you—Kade or baseball." Her tone was matter of fact.

"Why can't I have both?" I asked more to myself than her.

She scratched an eyebrow. "Maybe you can. Change their way of thinking. If this Triple-A team wants you, then negotiate a pregnancy into the contract. Make sure the contract has caveats for what you want. If they want you bad enough, then they'll meet your demands or meet you halfway."

"While that's great advice, I'm not sure a baseball organization will want me that badly."

Her idea made perfect sense, but I didn't think it was realistic. When the Dodgers were courting me right after I'd graduated college, their management team thought I was pregnant because I'd thrown up on the mound during a tryout. The end result was they went with another closer. At least that was what they'd told me. However, I believed they didn't want to take a chance on me because I was a female who came with a little more baggage, so to speak, than my male counterparts. She rolled her eyes. "You won't know until you ask."

Maybe so. But first I had a tough conversation with Kade ahead of me. If I didn't have him on my side, then asking for a pregnancy clause was a moot point.

CHAPTER 6
KADE

I found myself pacing the empty house again, waiting for Lacey. I'd dropped off Marcus after a two-hour conversation with him about how booze wasn't the answer to his problems. I'd also explained to him what my brothers and I had been through when we'd lost our sister and how each of us had found an outlet. Kross felt that ramming his fists into a punching bag helped him. I would've suggested to Marcus that music might be one avenue, which had helped Kody, but Marcus couldn't strum a guitar to save his life, according to Kody.

I peeked out the window in the living room, fuming. After Kross had told me what he'd heard about Lacey and a Triple-A team, it was all I could do to focus on Marcus.

Still, I'd told Lacey I would be a couple of hours. As much as I wanted to spend time with my wife, I felt Marcus needed help. I wasn't sure my advice would stick or resonate with him. After all, none of what I'd counseled him on in the past had seemed to change his rebellious nature.

Storm clouds moved in, darkening the sky as tree branches swayed back and forth along the side of the driveway.

Just as I was about to call her, I caught sight of her Mustang pulling in.

I padded over to the sprawling staircase and dropped down on the third step as my pulse settled for a beat.

The door opened, and a gust of wind followed Lacey in. "Hey," she said in a low voice, taming her windblown hair with her fingers.

I hopped up and rushed to her. "What happened?" Her eyes were red as though she'd been crying. I checked her arms and legs and everywhere skin was showing, but I didn't see any cuts.

She blinked once before pulling away and walking toward the kitchen.

My heart fell out of my chest. The last time she pulled away from me, she'd wanted nothing to do with me.

I trailed on her heels. "Lace?" She wasn't physically hurt, so someone had upset her.

She plunked her purse on the island and wiped the tears that had begun streaming down her face.

I had to touch her, hold her, console her, and tell her everything would be okay. At least I prayed like a motherfucker that we could get through whatever was bothering her. But when I approached her, she walked away again until she was on the other side of the island.

My heart stopped as memories bombarded me of the time in high school when we'd gotten into a major fight.

She got up and paced in front of the TV. "I've lived through finding the dead bodies of people I loved dearly. I've pushed hard in the last year to get where I am. I'm not perfect." She stuck her hands on her hips and pinned a deathly look on me. "I'll always have memories, nightmares, and symptoms of PTSD." Her face reddened. "How can I heal or face my fears when the one person I love, who's supposed to support me and help me, chooses to make the choices that are not his to make?"

I hopped off the couch and moved toward her. She backed away. I was about to lose it. I hated that she wouldn't let me touch her. I grabbed my hair with both my hands.

At that moment, I wasn't pulling on my hair. But I was tempted to punch my fist into our shiny stainless-steel fridge.

I inhaled through my nose, shoving my hands into the pockets of my jeans so Lacey wouldn't see me shaking. I wished I could say I wasn't a bundle of nerves, but the truth was I was fucking angry and gutted at her sudden coldness.

"If our marriage is over, tell me now." The words rolled off my tongue easily, which was stupid because I couldn't fathom why I would even think something like that. And we hadn't argued. We hadn't even spoken about her call with Tara yet.

Her jaw hit the granite top. "What!"

I pursed my lips as I settled against the copper sink. I had to have something to keep me upright because my knees were shaking. "You heard me." My voice didn't sound like my own.

She shuddered, licking her lips. "Why would you even think that?"

I shrugged. "Why won't you let me touch you? If you recall, the last time you wouldn't let me touch you, you stormed out of my house, and not long after that, you broke up with me."

Her eyes went wide. "You don't forget the smallest of details. Do you?"

"Not when they stop my heart from beating and surely not when it comes to you." I knew every single detail about Lacey Maxwell.

Her eyes slid shut for a second. "I'm sorry. I have something to tell you that will make you upset."

"About you playing Triple-A," I said.

She reared back. "How do you know? Did you talk to Tara?"

"Kross told me. He overheard some players from the Pawtucket Red Sox who were at the gym. They dropped your name and Triple-A."

Her beautiful features were scrunched in every direction. "But only Tara knows."

"Apparently not. But the bigger issue is what does this mean for starting our family?"

Shaking her head, she dashed a tear away with her fingers. "I don't know."

I pushed off the sink and planted my hands on the island that stood between us. "Lace, I'm not waiting another two years or three or five or ten to have a family. I'm sorry, baby. I'm not budging on this." Somehow, I'd managed to say all of that in a calm tone.

She jutted out her chin defiantly. "So you're not supporting my career any longer? Is that what you're saying?"

I dragged my hands through my hair as thunder boomed outside. I felt as though my heart beat with it. "We have a plan, Lace. That plan starts next year. That's as long as I'm willing to wait."

She sucked in a sharp breath. "Or what?" Her nostrils flared, anger jumping off her by leaps and bounds.

"Then I guess you need to figure out what's more important—us or baseball." Again, my tone was even. My pulse, not so much. The damn beat of my heart was pounding in my ears.

She worried her bottom lip. "And if I choose baseball?"

I pushed out a shoulder. "Then I guess we don't want the same things."

Her lips trembled. "So you're saying we're done?"

I sighed heavily before clenching my teeth. I would die a quick death if I ever lost Lacey. She'd been my rock since I'd met her. I couldn't imagine life without her. But if kids and a big family wasn't something she wanted, then I wasn't sure what I would do.

"You've always said you wanted kids, Lace. Why the shift in that?"

She puffed out air. "I do want kids, Kade. But I also want to play baseball. I've worked my ass off to get where I am today. You know as well as I do that the older I get, the fewer chances I'll have to play ball. I can't take off a year or two to have a baby and then expect to return and pick up where I left off. Teams wouldn't support that or sign me."

I locked my jaw. "Do you want to have a baby at forty years old?" My voice was no longer calm but shaky. "And we decided on at least four kids. When will that happen?"

A tear slid down her cheek. "I don't know. I just don't know."

Silence filled the spacious kitchen as she stared at the counter and I stared at her.

Thunder crashed, followed by the crack of lightning.

My gut twisted in several directions at the thought that she would pick baseball. I would die instantly if she did. Sure, I was being dramatic. But I loved the woman more than I loved anyone else or anything in this fucking world.

It's simple, man. If she picks baseball, then she doesn't want a family.

That scared the fuck out of me. Suddenly, I couldn't breathe. I felt as though fire streamed down my throat and burned a hole in my stomach.

I needed air... or a shot of hard liquor. I wasn't one to drown my sorrows or problems in booze like Marcus. But I was beginning to realize maybe booze was the key. My way of channeling my emotions had been working on old cars, which I rarely did. I'd barely had time for much as a teenager. I'd been the brother and son who took care of my siblings and mom. I'd been the one to shove all the pain and heartache down a dark hole and lock it up tightly. If I were being honest, Lacey had been my outlet. She'd been the one to make my heart whole again.

But at that moment while we were both in our own heads, my heart fucking hurt.

"I need some time alone," she whispered, still not meeting my gaze. "I'm going to see my dad." She started to walk out.

I rushed up to her and cocooned her in my arms. No way was she walking away from me.

She struggled to get free, albeit weakly.

"Lace, please don't break my heart." My voice cracked.

She stiffened and looked up at me with so much turmoil swirling in those meadow-green eyes that I thought I would lose my shit right then and there.

"I'll be back later tonight." She pushed out of my hold and left, taking my heart with her.

CHAPTER 7
LACEY

I curled up on a chair in the sunroom, listening to the rain pitter-patter on the glass roof, a sound that was soothing. I let my mind wander as I stared out into the backyard.

The copse of trees swayed from side to side.

Thunder boomed.

Lightning split the sky.

Suddenly, déjà vu hit me out of nowhere. I couldn't help but remember the time I'd sat in that very room with a thunderstorm in full gear, brooding over a fight I'd had with Kade. Back then, I'd been so angry with him, just like I was now. He'd made me so darn mad thinking I would leave him, and I couldn't see past that. I was also confused and angry with myself. I didn't want to break his heart.

I tried to put myself in his shoes, but if he were playing baseball, we wouldn't be arguing over when we would start a family. Sure, I wanted kids, but I also wanted to play ball.

Argh!

I would ruin my marriage if I didn't come to a decision. But if I did what I wanted, then I had a strong feeling that Kade wasn't going to hang around.

Nonsense. The man loves you to death. The man would die for you. You just have to come to a mutual decision. Maybe if the Triple-A team is interested, then only sign a one-year contract.

Surely, Kade would agree to extend our plans by one more year. The problem, though, was that I knew myself. I knew if I played, I wouldn't want to stop.

I tapped on Tara's name.

She answered on the first ring. "Lacey, aren't you supposed to be loving on that man of yours?"

I didn't share my personal life with Tara all that much. We talked but mostly about my career, although she knew family was important to me. "Do you think we can negotiate a pregnancy or two into a contract with the Iowa Cubs?"

Silence reigned over the line as the rain outside came down in sheets.

"Tara, are you still there?" I checked my screen to make sure the call hadn't dropped given the storm raging outside.

"I'm here. But..."

Yeah, I'd figured there was a "but" coming.

"You're forging a new path in this industry," she said. "But you knew going in that teams are frigid about a woman. I don't know that negotiating anything other than time and money is prudent with a new team."

I threw my head back. "Why is it so difficult to want a family and play ball? Don't answer that."

"Lacey, enjoy your break. Love on your hot husband. Let me do my job."

"Does that mean you'll talk to the Cubs about adding in a pregnancy clause of some sort?" I didn't know how it worked or how they would even word it. After all, there was a Pregnancy Discrimination Act. So maybe we didn't have to bring up the subject at all.

"It means not to worry about the Cubs. And I've told you that if you got pregnant in the middle of a season, then it's not going to end your career."

She had told me that in one of our meetings, but I hadn't believed her then, and I didn't now. Besides, I wasn't ready to find out how a team would react, despite a contract, which wasn't ironclad anyway.

"Lacey, don't let baseball ruin your marriage. We'll talk when you return to Portland. And if I speak with the Cubs before then, I'll call."

I sighed heavily. "I need both baseball and Kade, Tara. The last thing I want to do is disappoint my husband. But I don't want to lose all the blood, sweat, and tears I've put into baseball." I had to say that one last time even though she knew.

"We'll talk soon." The line went dead.

I rested my head against the chair when footsteps clobbered on the wood floor in the hall. I flew upright, my pulse off the charts. "Dad," I called.

The closer I crept toward the door, the harder my heart rammed against my ribs, and the faster my past reared its ugly head. The air left my lungs as a buzzing sound started in my ears. My PTSD was kicking in, something that hadn't happened since college. But I shouldn't have been surprised. The house held some dark memories with break-ins and even someone chasing me through the woods out back. Barry Weeks, a boy who'd befriended me, had thought I'd killed his father. But that feat had gone to the Boston SWAT team when Barry's father was a beat away from driving a knife into me.

I quickly poked my head out into the hall. A nightlight illuminated the dim space, but no one was there.

Icy fear washed through my veins. "Dad," I called again. He'd gone to Florida on business, but maybe he'd come home early.

"Lacey." Kade's voice dried the fear dripping from me, even more so when he came around the corner from the family room.

I'd never been so happy to see him in all my life.

He strutted toward me as though he was on a mission. I imagined he was. Kade Maxwell was always on a mission to make sure I wasn't hurt or being chased, kidnapped, or killed. I couldn't blame him. We'd had some tense times when my grandfather, who'd been head of the Italian Mafia in Los Angeles, had put a hit out on me. His reason had been to use me as bait to get a ledger that he'd thought my dad had.

I slapped a hand over my heart, hoping to slow it down.

Kade's eyes were wide. "Are you okay?"

"I'm fine." My voice cracked.

He wrapped his arms around me. "You let me be the judge of that." Then he lifted me in his arms and carried me into the sunroom. "You're not walking away from us." He set us down on the chair with me in his lap.

I hooked an arm around his neck. "Who said I was walking away? I just wanted a moment to think."

"Then think in a room in our house. Fuck, it's big enough for you to hide." He waved his hand outward. "You don't need to be driving in this crap weather."

I traced the pad of my finger over his lips as my anger started to wane. I couldn't stay mad at him, and he was right—our house was big enough to find a quiet spot to think, but I'd wanted to see my dad. He always gave me great advice. But I hadn't known he was out of town until I'd gotten there.

"Careful, Lace. I bite." Kade's tone was hard and serious.

"Then bite. I'm not afraid of you."

"But you are afraid to talk about kids?"

I stiffened.

He raised an eyebrow. "See? I mention kids, and you go ramrod straight. Look, we're not leaving here until we talk or yell or shout. I don't give a fuck what."

I slumped. "You're bossy."

He chuckled, losing all that tension in his jaw.

I placed my fingers on his chin and guided him to look at me. "I'm sorry. I'm scared. I'm confused, and you can't be mad because I want to play ball and spit out kids." Not exactly a nice way to say that last part, but I wanted to get a better smile from him. I wanted us both to relax before we talked about anything.

"I'm an idiot for thinking you would walk away from us. Please forgive me." So much emotion swam in his copper depths. Those same eyes had sucked me in when I'd met him for the first time seven years ago.

I would never forget that day. The bright lights in that high school parking lot had hit his face just perfectly. His copper eyes had sparkled. His long lashes had fluttered, and I remembered wondering how it would feel to have his long lashes skimming over my face or anywhere on my body.

Butterfly kisses.

He traced circles on my bare leg, eliciting a string of goose bumps. "Penny for your thoughts." His voice was husky and downright panty-melting.

I captured his lips, pushing my tongue through until we were in a heated kiss. All that tension fell away, and before I knew what was happening, I was straddling him while his hands were on the move over my body—my waist, my breasts, my ass, everywhere.

The pounding of the rain became our music as the drops pinged off the glass roof of the sunroom.

He threaded his fingers through my hair, tugging my head back before he began kissing my neck.

"Mr. Steel is growing," I said through a moan.

"I need to be inside you." His voice was raspy.

He didn't have to say another word. In a flash, I was naked, standing before him.

He raked his gaze up then down, slow and sure. I felt like he was kissing every part of my body.

He tore off his shirt. "You're more beautiful than the day we met."

I licked my lips as I admired my gorgeous husband. The man was all muscle with dips and valleys on his upper torso. But the one area that always got me right where it counted were the hearts tattooed on his chest—five of them. Four of the hearts represented his siblings. The one that sat above them had my name inked inside, and that was the reason happy tears burned my eyes.

"You know we have a problem."

One of his eyebrows went up. "Oh?"

"I'm naked, and you're not."

He remedied that in two seconds flat. As we both stood naked and facing each other with the rain pouring down, all the tension, problems, life, and anything or anyone who could get in our way didn't matter.

He erased the short distance between us, bowed his head, pinched one of my nipples, and leaned into my ear. "I'm going to fuck you until the sun comes up."

I shivered in delight. "I love when you talk dirty. But first, you have to catch me." I ran out of the sunroom, giggling like I was a teenager again.

He let out a belly laugh. "You know I'm faster than you."

It was my turn to laugh as I banked a corner in the hallway that led upstairs. "Maybe. But can you find me?" Of course he could. My dad's house wasn't as big as our new home. The game wasn't about whether

Kade could find me or not. It was more about letting go of our problems and having fun for one night.

My bare feet slapped on the steps. I knew he could hear me.

"I always find you," he said as his voice drew closer.

CHAPTER 8
KADE

I took my time climbing the stairs to where the bedrooms were located. With each step, my pulse ticked higher as my cock got harder. We hadn't played hide-and-seek in a while, and I missed this game with her.

The house was quiet except for the creaking noise of the stairs.

"Lacey, I'm close," I teased.

I didn't think she was in the bedrooms, but she had a habit of hiding in the bathtub.

I squeezed my dick for no reason but to distract me from what I was about to do to her when I caught her.

When I reached the top landing, I listened for the slightest of noises but was met with dead silence.

All the doors leading into the bedrooms and a bathroom were open.

I stalked down the hall, poking my head into one bedroom. It was empty. I went in and checked the closet.

I stood in the middle of her old room, which was now a storage of sorts for her old man's files. I listened closely and grinned. "Lace, baby, I know you're up here."

I proceeded to the next room. After looking into the other rooms, I still hadn't found her.

Standing in the bathroom, I rubbed my rock-hard dick, trying to think.

After she'd torn out of the sunroom, I could've sworn I heard her climb the stairs.

Again, I listened intently, but the pitter-patter of the raindrops on the skylight muffled my ability to hear anything else in the house.

I let go of my dick and made my way downstairs. When I reached the bottom, a faint moan tickled my ears.

"Lace," I called. "You better not be touching yourself, at least not without me watching you."

She giggled.

Son of a bitch. She had somehow fooled me into thinking she'd come upstairs.

My legs kicked into gear. If I didn't get inside her, I just might lose my load in my hand. I rounded the staircase, trudged down the hall, and came to an abrupt halt.

"You looking for me?" Lacey asked innocently. She stood in front of the fireplace, legs spread, fingers circling her clit while the others were massaging her breast.

I grabbed my dick as hard as I could, stroking as I stepped toward her. My balls had disappeared, and any second I was a goner.

I got within a foot of her then pounced. I gripped her waist and carried her to the couch, practically falling onto a cushion.

She giggled relentlessly as I tried to push inside her as fast as I could.

"You think this is funny?" I asked as pain laced every word. Sure, it was fucking delicious pain, but man, I was trying so stinking hard to hold back. I wasn't going to last. I was a fucking teenager again, ready to orgasm over the sight of her tits and ass.

She maneuvered her body expertly as though she'd straddled me a thousand times. True, she had, but the moment I was inside her and she was gripping my cock, I threw my head back and groaned so loud, I wouldn't be surprised if the neighbors could hear me over the storm.

She laughed, a sound that only served to make me hornier than I'd ever been. But then she hopped off me.

My head whipped up, my jaw fell open, and my eyes bugged out of my head. "What the fuck?" But those words died a quick death as she dropped to her knees.

She licked her lips. "I want to play."

Before I had a chance to nod, she was sucking me so hard, I saw stars.

My hands dove in her hair. "That's it, baby, harder."

Her tongue swirled around the tip of my cock, her hands pumping me. Then she took me deep, and I practically bucked off the couch.

"Fuck, Lace. I can't hold it any longer."

"Let go, baby. I got you." Her words were mumbled as she sucked me off until I was screaming her fucking name. As I came down out of the clouds, she crawled onto my lap.

I crashed my mouth to hers, my tongue snaking in, taking, tasting, and devouring.

She eased back, a smile emerging. "That was fun."

I massaged her breasts. "Which part?"

"Hide-and-seek. I had you fooled."

"My brain wasn't firing on all cylinders," I teased.

She giggled. "Only Mr. Steel."

I sucked on her nipple.

"Kade." Her tone lost that playfulness.

I leaned back to find she had a serious expression painted on.

"I don't want baseball to come between us. I'm scared."

Whoa! I cupped her cheeks. "We'll work through this." I would do anything and everything to make sure we did. "I have to be honest. I'm scared too. I'm afraid you'll pick baseball over us."

She pressed her forehead to mine, and a tear slid down her cheek. "You're my everything."

I could hear a "but" in her tone.

She brushed her lips over mine. "Don't ever think that our marriage is over." She bit my bottom lip. "You made me so mad. I would die for you, Kade Maxwell."

"I'm sorry. I was an ass to think that."

She nodded.

"I was thinking on the drive over here."

She pulled away, regarding me with an eager expression.

I swiped a lone tear off her cheek with the pad of my thumb.

My beautiful Lacey.

"Since you started playing for the Sea Dogs, we haven't spent enough time together. We've both been going in different directions. It's time I lock up the house and spend the rest of your season with you in Portland."

Her jaw came unhinged. "Really?" She squealed, a sound that made my dick jerk beneath her ass.

Her excitement quickly died, though. "How does that solve the kiddie problem?"

I trailed my fingers up her torso, then down, then back up. "It doesn't exactly. But we just need the time together. So tell me about the offer." I wasn't exactly sure she had an offer, but considering she'd spoken to Tara, I would put money on that.

She sucked in her bottom lip. "The Iowa Cubs are interested in me." Her green eyes lit up like an airport runway. "A Triple-A team. Can you believe that?" Her smile was radiant.

My heart soared despite my own desperation to start a family. I couldn't deny her that opportunity. I loved her too much to see her lose that smile or that gleam in her eyes when she talked about baseball or played the damn game.

Baseball was Lacey.

Lacey was baseball.

She should be able to play and have a family. She should live her dream.

I grinned so wide, my lips hurt. "That's fantastic news. You're ready for the big leagues."

"Yeah? You're really happy for me?"

I lost my grin. "Why would you ask me that?"

She flattened her hands on my chest then rubbed her fingers lightly over my heart tattoos. "You want kids like yesterday."

"Baby, I want you more," I said as sure as the rain was still coming down. "We'll figure things out. I want you to be happy, Lace. I want to see that smile on your face when you get ready to play the game. I want to hear the giddiness in your voice when you talk baseball. Above all else, I love the crap out of you, and I'm with you one hundred percent." Sure, part of me was sad and gutted that we might not be able to start our family next year like we'd planned. But I would be even more devastated if my wife wasn't happy.

"I love you so much, it hurts sometimes. I feel selfish that I want to live my dream when yours is to have kids."

"Nonsense. We're in this together. Remember? For better or worse. As I said, we'll figure it out."

She gave me a weak smile. "I do want kids more than anything. I just want you to know that."

I dragged a finger down and over one of her breasts. "I know you do. And we'll have them."

She sighed. "I asked Tara if she could negotiate a pregnancy addendum into a contract." She pushed out a shoulder. "I don't know if she can, but companies give their employees maternity leave. So why not a baseball team?" She sounded like she was trying to convince herself it was a no-brainer.

Hope bloomed in my chest for the first time. Maybe it was that easy. After all, Lacey shouldn't be penalized in her field just because she wanted to have a kid.

"We should look at renting a house in Portland," I said.

"You're full of surprises." Her voice hitched. "But let's wait until next year to do that. The season will be over in a couple of months or so. It doesn't make sense to get a house for that short of a time."

I pulled her to me.

Whatever fate had in store for us, I was ready. Because I would die for this woman. I would give my soul to the devil just to see her happy.

CHAPTER 9
LACEY

The All-Star break had come and gone, and after a month of being away from Kade, I was dying to see him. He'd had every intention of returning with me, but I'd wanted him to get a checkup before he packed his bags. He'd had two migraines while I'd been home, and that was one too many for me, especially because the second one had knocked him on his ass during my last day home, which scared the crap out of me. All I kept thinking was that he had another tumor, and this time, what if it wasn't benign?

I leaned against a brick building outside a quaint Italian restaurant and tapped Kade's name on my phone.

The city of Portland was hopping with traffic and people coming and going from restaurants and small shops that lined both sides of downtown.

"Are you close?" I asked when the line connected.

"I finally got off the highway." His husky voice settled the nerves I'd had all day worrying about his doctor's appointment. "I should be there in about ten minutes."

"Did the doc say anything?"

"I only had my checkup this morning, Lace. He said he would call as soon as he got the results. Don't worry." His tone had a feather softness on the last words. I knew he was trying not to worry me. But that was like telling him not to worry about me.

For the last few weeks, my stomach had been in knots. Hell, it still was. My mind had been consumed with what-ifs. What if he did have a malignant tumor? What if we didn't have time to have kids?

I'd been thinking I should put my career on hold and do everything in my power to get pregnant. I was selfish. I was the one living my dream, and Kade wasn't living his.

"Is Tara there yet?" he asked.

I wanted to say I didn't care about Tara or the news she had for me. But I did want to hear how her talks had gone with the Iowa Cubs. In all honesty, I wasn't as eager to know at the moment, as I would have been otherwise. If my husband wasn't in good health, then nothing else trumped him.

"She's stuck in the same traffic."

"So has she told you how her meeting went?" Kade asked.

"All she said was we'll talk at dinner." I'd tried to get more out of her, but she'd had another call coming in, and I'd had a meeting with my manager earlier that day.

"I'm pulling into a parking garage. See you in a minute." The line clicked off.

I sent Tara a text: *Kade and I will be outside the restaurant.*

Tara responded quickly: *I'm taking an Uber from the hotel. I should be there in a few minutes.*

I lowered my phone, scanning up and down the street. A parking garage was located one block up, and another sat one block down. I didn't know which one Kade was parking in.

The bell on the door dinged, announcing a middle-aged couple leaving the Italian restaurant. As they did, a spicy aroma floated out, causing my stomach to growl. I usually didn't eat much before a game, thanks in part to my nerves, so I was famished. My mouth was watering for a plate of ravioli or spaghetti.

As I watched the couple walk down the street, my gaze drifted past them, and I smiled when I spotted my hunky husband jogging toward me. Before my brain could catch up with my body, my legs were moving until I was jumping into his arms as though we hadn't seen each other in years.

His hands dove into my hair, and our lips locked in a heated kiss.

A horn blew, snapping us back to reality. I slid down his muscled body, feeling Mr. Steel along the way.

I couldn't help but giggle. "I've missed you," I said a little breathlessly.

"Is there any way we can bag dinner with Tara?" he asked. "I need to be inside you." His warm breath fanned over my ear, causing hot lava to pinch my cheeks.

As much as I would love to reschedule with Tara, I couldn't. She had driven up from Boston to meet with us. It was only polite to see our meeting through.

I shook my head. "We won't stay long."

Kade looked around. "We could go down that alley across the street while we wait for her."

I playfully slapped him. "I'm all for an adventure, but Tara is getting out of the car." I flicked my head at the black Mercedes.

She dashed up onto the sidewalk with a smile that didn't reach her brown eyes. "I'm exhausted and hungry. Sorry I'm late." She glanced at Kade. "Do you know what happened on the highway exactly?"

"Some eighteen-wheeler jackknifed and ended up on its side," he said.

That was why Tara and Kade hadn't been at my game earlier.

The three of us walked into the cozy and elegant Italian restaurant.

Tara took the lead and spoke to the young blond hostess.

Kade leaned into my ear. "Let's not linger too long, please. I'm tired as hell."

I rolled my eyes. "You just want sex."

"Sue me."

The restaurant was dim and quiet with several empty tables. I shouldn't have been surprised since the dinnertime had come and gone.

The hostess placed us at a table by the window. Then she handed each of us a menu.

No sooner had she left than a waiter in his twenties came over. He took our drink orders and spouted out the specials.

When I finally had a chance to sip some water, some of my muscles loosened but only because Kade was sitting next to me with his arm draped over the back of my chair. His presence always gave me the sense that I could handle anything.

But when I regarded Tara, my stomach churned. I'd known her for over two years, and I knew she had bad news for me. When she smoothed a hand over her short brown bob, she confirmed my suspicions. That small act was her tell that she was about to deliver news I wouldn't like.

She set her wide brown eyes on me as she cleared her throat. "The Iowa Cubs have decided on another pitcher for their roster next year." Tara interlaced her fingers as she set her hands on the table. She was the type of person who didn't beat around the bush.

I liked that about her, and even though my excitement about playing Triple-A ball had waned a tad, the news still stung like an angry hornet.

"You could've told her that on the phone," Kade said.

"Not my style," Tara replied. "I don't like to deliver bad news on the phone. Lacey, you don't seem disappointed." She sipped her water. "Why?"

I swallowed thickly and regarded Kade briefly. "I've had a lot of time to think since the All-Star break." I placed my hand on Kade's thigh, still keeping my eyes on Tara. "My marriage comes first."

"Lace," Kade said. "We talked about this. I want you to play ball."

I batted my eyelashes at my husband. "I know you do. But I also want kids. And the more I think about the talk we had, the more I realize that we'll be in a never-ending cycle with my career. If it's not the Iowa Cubs, it could be some other team. Honestly, I really don't want to have kids at forty or later when I finally decide to retire."

Kade leaned in and kissed me on the temple. "Don't make an important decision like this because of me."

"I'm not. I'm making it for us." In that moment, looking into the gleam and love in his copper eyes, I didn't want anything else other than to please him. He'd endured so much with me, and I hadn't done much other than love him with all my heart. Sure, he might think that my love for him was all that mattered, but in my mind, it wasn't. A marriage was more than love. It was building a life together that included the wants and needs of both of us. We needed to meet each other halfway. I hadn't done that.

Tara cleared her throat. "Well, the other reason I drove through hell to get here..."

Kade and I swung our gazes to her.

"I've spoken to the Sea Dogs. I wanted to test the waters on whether they're interested in re-signing you when your contract is up next year." That time, her smile did reach her eyes. "I'm happy to say they don't want to lose you. So I broached the subject of what if you got pregnant, and they have no issues with that. However, they would only sign you on a yearly basis."

My jaw hit the table despite her last sentence. I would prefer a two- or three-year deal, but I understood that the organization wouldn't want to tie up their assets. After all, a pregnancy would put me on the disabled list for at least two months or more unless I timed it so I would deliver in the off-season.

Kade just stared at her. "That's the best news I've heard."

Hearing the excitement in his voice gave me goose bumps, and for the moment, everything was right in my world.

CHAPTER 10
KADE

Daylight wormed its way through a slit in the room-darkening curtains that covered one wall of the hotel room. For the last three weeks, we'd been on the road all over New England for Lacey's away games, and I was tired of packing and unpacking and eating at restaurants or ordering room service. Although staying in at night with Lacey wrapped around me after we ate dinner had been nothing short of amazing, even when she passed out from exhaustion. The fact that we were together was enough to make my heart soar, and I realized that I should've been traveling with her more, taking care of her more, pampering her more.

Our life was about us, and "us" included baseball. I realized in the time I'd been on the road with her that she was tougher than I even knew. She kept up a grueling schedule during the season, and I admired her even more than I had when I'd first met her.

I rubbed my eyes as a dull headache loomed. My test results had come back negative with no tumors on the scan. The doc had said I was a normal person who would get headaches on occasion and even migraines. He'd prescribed some migraine medication just in case.

I chalked up my headaches to stress, and the doc agreed.

"Stress can spur one on," he'd said. "Just make sure you schedule your physicals on an annual basis." Like I'd had time to do anything in the last year while caring for four teenagers and building a house at the same time. As much as I might complain about my cousins, I'd rather enjoyed having them at the house.

Speaking of my cousins, Kody had informed me that Marcus had been helping him at the club during the day—washing floors and stocking shelves. Apparently, Marcus was still brooding, but Kody hadn't seen him drunk since the day we'd found him passed out on the stage. Kross had spent some time with Marcus as well. And according to Kross, Marcus was a natural in the ring.

Yawning, I turned onto my side to find Lacey wasn't in bed. So I climbed out, running my hand through my hair. As I was about to take a step, I heard her moaning, but it wasn't a good sound.

I bolted toward the bathroom. When I threw open the door, I sucked in a sharp breath.

Lacey was on her knees, hugging the toilet.

I squatted next to her, moving her hair off her shoulder, and felt her forehead, which was sweaty. But she showed no signs of a fever.

She glanced up at me with tired green eyes. She'd been quite depressed since receiving the news that the Iowa Cubs had decided to sign a newbie coming out of college.

"I'm old," Lacey had said. "My baseball days are numbered."

"Horse shit," I'd replied. "Look on the bright side. The Sea Dogs will work with you if you get pregnant."

"Maybe," she'd said. "But they won't re-sign me after that one-year contract is up. They're probably too afraid that I'll get pregnant again."

She wiped her mouth with the back of her hand. "I think it's something I ate. Maybe the crab cakes at dinner. They tasted a little funny, but I thought that was—" She whipped her head over the toilet and puked.

I grabbed a washcloth, doused it with cold water, and waited until she was finished. Then I patted her face, hoping the coolness of the cloth would help her.

She puffed out her cheeks and settled with her back against the tub. "I hope I can play today."

She was a relief pitcher. So it wasn't like she was starting. Her manager could always put in another relief pitcher. However, knowing Lacey, she wouldn't tell her manager she wasn't feeling well. She would just play. She was that stubborn when it came to baseball. She'd said on more than one occasion that she had to work harder than her male counterparts. I wouldn't disagree, but if she was sick, her performance would suffer, and so would the team.

I propped my hip against the counter. "Maybe you should call in sick."

She hugged her knees to her chest. "I don't have to be at the field for a few hours. I'll see how I feel later. Right now, I just want to crawl back into bed and rest."

That sounded good to me. I held out my hand. "Come on. We can snuggle." I wasn't working as hard as her, so I shouldn't have been tired, but I was.

She pushed to her feet on shaky legs. When she did, I lifted her in my arms and carried her to bed.

Then I kissed her on the forehead before cuddling up to her from behind.

Within minutes, her breathing became steady and even as she dozed off.

I lay there, trying to sleep, but my mind was in overdrive. Baseball season drained the energy out of her. Even when the season ended, it took her a month or more to finally relax, and just as she did, the season started up again. It was an endless cycle.

Lacey rolled over and slipped her leg in between mine, a position she loved when we snuggled. Just as she nuzzled her nose into my chest, she darted out of bed and ran for the bathroom. The sound of her puking again echoed in the quiet room.

I got up and dressed quickly. "I'll go find something for your nausea." I didn't wait for her to say anything as I grabbed the room key, my wallet, and my phone and hurried out.

Twenty minutes later when I returned, Lacey was curled up on the small loveseat in the sitting area, reading on her phone, while an ESPN announcer on the TV went through the highlights of the Red Sox game the night before.

I dropped down next to her, setting the bag of Pepto Bismol and bagels on the table along with the coffee I'd gotten at the hotel restaurant. "Feeling better?"

She looked somewhat pale but not as white as she had earlier. "I will be. By the way, my manager called. He wants the team in early for a meeting before we warm up."

"Are you sure you'll be fine?"

She shrugged. "I've played many times when I wasn't feeling well. I'm good."

In that moment, a memory flashed through my mind, and I was transported back to that day in high school when Lacey had been trying out for the boys' baseball team.

I sat in the stands at Kensington High, watching Lacey as she warmed up to face a batter. I fidgeted in my seat, breathing in and out, praying she would do okay. She'd been nervous as hell.

She threw her first pitch to the batter. The ball was wild, and the catcher fumbled to catch the ball.

Come on. You can do it, *I muttered to myself as the crowd watching held their breath too.*

The batter stepped out of the box, taking some practice swings, but my focus was on Lacey, who was puffing out her cheeks, blowing out breath after breath. Then when the batter was ready, Lacey wound up and let the ball fly. That time the pitch soared over the umpire, hitting the backstop with a thud as my heart followed suit.

My brother, Kelton, who was playing shortstop, ran up to Lacey.

My pulse thudded in my ears. I could feel her anxiety from where I sat.

Kelton and the catcher talked her down. She bobbed her head as everyone readied their positions.

I covered my mouth with my hands, holding all the air in my lungs as she set her stance. When she looked down at home plate, she froze as if she saw a ghost. Then in slow motion, her body fell forward as she blacked out.

"Kade, honey." Lacey's voice was distant as I slowly shed the memory of that day. She nibbled on my ear. "Where did you go?"

I shook my head to erase the sinking feeling in my stomach. "How's your PTSD?" We hardly talked about her disorder. Since her grandfather had passed, she hadn't had any symptoms, at least not that I knew of.

She knitted her brows. "Where did that come from?"

Lifting a shoulder, I relaxed back against the couch. "I had a flashback of you on the mound in high school when you blacked out."

Her mouth opened slightly. "Why? My nausea has nothing to do with my PTSD."

"But if you're not feeling well, your reflexes aren't sharp. You could get hit by a line drive or—"

She grasped my hand. "Stop worrying."

I wanted to tell her to stop being stubborn, but I didn't want to argue. I had to trust her. She knew her body better than me. On that note, my dick started to get hard, especially when I really took her in. Her nipples were poking out of her Sea Dogs T-shirt.

She followed my line of sight before she glanced up at me, biting her lip.

Sexy as hell.

Then in a flash, I was carrying her to bed, thinking only of the things I was about to do to her.

CHAPTER 11
KADE

I loved the game of baseball. I'd played in my freshman year of high school, but after that I had never played any more sports. I'd been the caretaker to my three brothers while Mom was in a mental health facility and Dad was working or out of town on a business trip. So my free time had been nonexistent.

But sitting in the stands for the last three weeks, I was getting burnt out on the game. The only exciting part for me was watching Lacey pitch, and on some nights, her manager didn't put her in. His choices of relief pitchers were all about strategy, the opposing team, the batters, and whether he needed a left-handed or right-handed pitcher.

I rested my elbows on my knees as the Sea Dogs took the field in the top of the eighth inning against the Hartford Yard Goats in Connecticut. After the game, I was tempted to zip home to Ashford to check on things. We really weren't that far, and we could get home and back before Lacey had to play the next day. Not that anything required my attention. I just wanted to see my folks and see how Kody was getting by managing The Cave.

The catcher's wife, who was sitting next to me, nudged me in the arm, shattering thoughts of home. "Your wife is taking the mound," Nan Bradley said.

I zeroed in on my baseball beauty as she twirled the ball in both hands, glancing around the field then over at me.

I grinned as she beamed and nodded.

"Newlyweds," Nan mumbled. "Oh, to be that young again."

I didn't know how old Nan was, but from what Lacey had told me and from what little I'd learned in my time in the stands, Nan and her husband, Steve, had been married for ten years. They had an eight-year-old daughter and lived in Portland year-round.

Nan was also extremely chatty and seemed to be the mother hen among the baseball spouses. I'd overheard her giving advice to one young spouse the other night about how the life of a baseball player was grueling and exciting all at the same time. But spouses needed to have an outlet while their husbands played the game.

I wasn't one to eavesdrop or gossip, but I'd zoned in on listening. I thought her advice had been good for me because sometimes I forgot how much work Lacey put into playing the game, which had been eye-opening over the last few weeks.

I stared at my wife, hoping she was feeling better than she had that morning. She'd promised me she didn't feel the need to puke when she left for the ballpark. I wasn't sure I believed her because she still looked pale to me.

Lacey threw several pitches, warming up as the infielders tossed the ball around, as did the outfielders.

"I'm in awe of her," Nan said.

I grinned proudly. "So am I." Lacey was an inspiration. I'd had a chance to see the girls, young and old, wait for her after a game for her autograph.

"My husband talks about Lacey all the time. He, too, thinks she's carving a great path for little girls. Our little girl wants to be Lacey when she grows up."

I couldn't lose the smile on my face if Nan paid me. I wanted our little girl or girls to be just like my wife too. I wanted them to be strong, vibrant, outgoing, and have every opportunity to live their dreams just like their mom.

Mom? I could hear our kids now, running around the house shouting for Mom or Dad. I grinned at that thought.

"When do you think you guys will have kids?" Nan asked.

The umpires got into position as the first batter approached the plate.

I angled my head at Nan. "Not sure." *Tomorrow if it were up to me.*

"My husband and I keep wondering when Lacey will get pregnant and how that will work for the team."

I found it interesting that Nan and her husband were thinking along those lines, and I was happy to hear that at least one of the players was already considering the possibility.

"What does Steve think of Lacey getting pregnant during the season?" Not that his opinion mattered, but if some of the team had been talking about it, I was curious what they thought.

She fiddled with a chain around her neck as her red lips parted into a smile. "Steven and I agree that whenever Lacey gets pregnant, she should still be allowed to play up until she can't. She's in great shape. So physically, it's doable. I know women athletes like runners who get pregnant and still play their sport."

I sighed quietly. As much as the Sea Dogs might be onboard to support Lacey with a pregnancy, it would be interesting to see how they would actually react. Maybe Lacey was right. Maybe the team wouldn't re-sign her after she gave birth. As much as I would like to think the organization would support Lacey, baseball was all about the bottom line. If Lacey couldn't play, then they would lose money.

Nan waved her fan in front of her. The weather was humid, and the night air was dead with no breeze. "If you time it right, you could have the baby in the off-season. Then she's ready to go when spring training rolls around."

I grinned because Nan had a plan for us all figured out. "Have you shared any of this with Lacey?" Lacey had had dinner with Nan and her husband on occasion. Maybe hearing those thoughts from someone other than me would give my wife some hope that she could have baseball and a family.

Nan nodded. "I think Lacey is afraid to go down that path. She shared with me that she's concerned the team will drop her. But they can't. If she's under contract, she's locked in, and besides, with the Pregnancy Discrimination Act, no company or team can just end her contract without a good enough reason."

I recalled that when Lacey had tried out for the Dodgers right after college, one of the scouts had told me that very thing. And while the laws were in place, my wife was afraid the team would use some excuse to let her go.

I glanced out at Lacey, who was winding up her pitch. When she released the ball, the batter swung and missed.

A group of young girls sitting off to our left shouted Lacey's name, cheering her on.

"It doesn't matter where we go. Everyone loves her," Nan said.

I wasn't surprised. Lacey was becoming an icon in the industry and forging a new path for girls of all ages.

"We do want kids, so I'm hoping we can get there one day," I said to Nan as if she were my counselor.

She patted my leg. "You will."

I knew we would. The question was when.

We settled in to watch the game. Lacey struck out the first batter in four pitches. She wiped the sweat from her brow with the sleeve of her uniform. She circled the mound, dug her foot into the dirt, glanced around the field, and shook her head. Her shoulders hunched. Then she stilled, lowered her head, and puffed out her cheeks.

A boulder dropped into my stomach. Something was wrong.

"Is she okay?" Nan asked.

"She wasn't feeling well this morning," I said almost to myself.

"It's probably the humidity. It's been awful the last few days," Nan added.

True. I was hoping the game would end now so we could get back to the air-conditioned hotel room.

She cocked her leg and released the ball. The pitch flew over the umpire's head. The ball hit the backstop with a thud.

For the second time that day, her tryouts in high school flashed like lightning in front of me.

I stiffened, swallowed the sand in my throat, and prayed she wasn't about to puke. She'd puked during her tryouts with the Dodgers, mainly because of nerves. Surely she didn't have any nerves now. She'd been playing the game with the same team for two years.

Steve jogged out to the mound to hand her the ball. They exchanged some words, then he resumed his position behind home plate.

The batter stepped into the box, readied his stance, and waited for Lacey to pitch.

Lacey settled in, taking inventory of the field and the runner at first base. She eyed the batter, home plate, and the catcher. As she wound up to release the ball, her body became a rag doll.

Before I could blink, she was on the ground.

CHAPTER 12
LACEY

I winced, opening my eyes, but a haze of cloudiness shrouded my view. Muffled voices trickled into my ears, and I recognized Kade's. His husky and panicked voice was unmistakable. I'd heard him panic before. I'd heard him freak out before.

It took me a minute to realize I wasn't upright but on a stretcher. Bright lights shone down from overhead. I blinked several times to orient my vision. I raised my hand, trying to sit up, but the dizziness was too much. "Kade?" His name was barely a whisper, maybe because my throat was as dry as the Sahara Desert.

"Yes, baby. I'm here," he said before his beautiful face came into view, albeit a little blurry.

"What happened?" I swished around the saliva in my mouth.

"Room five," said a nearby female voice.

Then Kade's handsome mug was gone, and I was moving, or maybe my head was spinning too much.

I shut my eyes tightly and thought real hard. But before I could pull up a memory, nurses were surrounding me, hooking up an IV, and pressing pads to my chest. Then something was squeezing the hell out of my arm.

"Blood pressure is still low," one of the nurses said.

I was in a haze as they tended to me hurriedly, as if I were a heartbeat away from dying.

A pretty brunette nurse with wide hazel eyes smiled at me. "I'm Steph, one of the ER nurses. Can you tell me your name?"

I licked my lips. "Lacey Maxwell."

"Can you tell me what happened?" Steph asked as her partner stuck the IV needle into the back of my hand.

I winced at the sting of the needle as images of me on the mound filled my vision. "One minute, I was ready to pitch, and the next, a wave of dizziness hit me out of nowhere."

The nurse who pricked me regarded me with crystal-blue eyes. "I'm Blaire. Are you dizzy or nauseated at all?"

"Just dizzy. Where's my husband?" I lifted my head to search the room but couldn't find Kade.

"I'm here, baby."

I rolled my head around like I was working out a kink in my neck. But the act only served to make the room spin. "I feel sick."

Blaire patted my arm. "You should start to feel better once we get fluids in you. You're probably severely dehydrated."

"She was puking this morning," Kade said from somewhere in the room.

A machine beeped behind me.

"Bad food," I added.

"Lacey," Blaire said. "I'm going to take some blood, and Steph is going to ask you some questions. All of this is routine. Okay?"

I nodded. "I need to get back to the team, though."

Steph tossed a look behind her, flicking her head in a swift move.

Within a second, Kade was standing at the bottom of the bed. He grinned, although his smile didn't reach his eyes. "The game is over."

"What? How long have I been here? Did we win?" My pulse quickened. My manager was probably going nuts. My teammates were probably concerned too. Suddenly, my cheeks heated. I'd passed out on the field during a freaking game in front of a packed stadium.

Mortified was the perfect word to describe how I felt underneath the cloudiness that seemed to want to stick to my brain and skin.

"You were just brought in." Blaire pricked me again, that time taking blood from my arm.

"The team won," Kade said in a flat tone, like he didn't even care.

I imagined he didn't. He liked baseball, but he didn't live and breathe the game like I did.

I blew out a breath. We'd been up by two runs when I took the mound. Still, I didn't want to be responsible for a loss.

Kade swung his gaze between the nurses. "What would cause low blood pressure?"

Steph typed on a computer that was bolted to a rolling cart. "Dehydration and diet are a couple of factors."

The *tap, tap, tap* of the keys was in sync with the beat of my pulse as I continued to stare at my handsome husband. "There's nothing to worry about."

He angled his head and gave me one of his blank expressions that drove me batshit crazy. Although I knew him as well as he knew me. He was silently shouting all kinds of cuss words in his head. His internal war probably went something like, *I shouldn't have let her leave for the field. I should've insisted that she call in sick.*

The problem was that players didn't call in sick. If for some reason I couldn't play, I still had to show up to the field. Then the team doctor would assess me before any decisions were made about whether to put me in the lineup. Regardless, I hadn't felt dizzy or sick when I'd arrived at the field.

Kade only grinned. I could sense he was waiting for us to be alone so he could vent his frustration. Not to mention he wanted to hear from the nurses or a doctor that nothing was seriously wrong with me.

I suspected I was tired, stressed, and dehydrated. I swear that the food I'd eaten for dinner the night before hadn't tasted good.

"Can someone let the team know I'm okay?" I said more than asked.

"I will," Kade replied, gripping the edge of the bed like he was holding on for dear life.

"I'm fine, Kade," I felt compelled to say again.

A phone rang. Kade pulled out his and lifted it to his ear as he walked out.

I sighed heavily as though he'd just given me oxygen that I desperately needed.

"He's worried." Blaire flicked her gaze at me as she finished taking my blood. Then she zipped out of the room.

"He worries too much," I mumbled.

If Steph heard me, she didn't say a word but rather dove into her many questions. How many times had I puked that morning? Had I been nauseated every morning? What had I eaten last night? The list went on and on and on to include my medical history.

She rolled the computer away and stood at my bedside. "Final question. Do you think you could be pregnant?"

My mouth dropped open. "What? No! I'm using an IUD."

She deadpanned. "Have you missed a period?"

Then Becca's words came flashing back. *"IUDs are not one hundred percent preventive. You know that, right?"*

A shudder tiptoed up my spine. *Pregnant?*

"I hardly get one," I whispered only because my voice was nonexistent. *I can't be pregnant.* I started counting nine months out in my head. That would have me delivering in April when baseball season officially started. I was happy the Sea Dogs would support me, but I wasn't ready to have a child now. I wanted to finish out my contract at least. Maybe if I got pregnant midway through next season, I could deliver when baseball finished in the fall. Then I could play without having to go on the disabled list. If I could manage that, the team would see that I could play and be a mom without any interruptions.

My face burned hot and bright as tears readied themselves to spill at any second.

"Makes sense," she said. "Women athletes have been known not to have periods. The blood tests will tell us. Sit tight."

Sit tight? I wanted to laugh. How in the world could I sit idle while I waited for test results?

"I can't be pregnant," I muttered.

Steph had just reached the curtain that was used as a door to the room. "Rest for now. The doctor will be in soon."

A scream sat on my tongue as I thought back to the last time I'd had my period. I never kept track. And since I had switched from the pill to an IUD, my periods were much lighter.

I took in a few deep breaths to calm my pulse, which was all over the place. My brain was on overdrive. How was I going to deal with a pregnancy and baseball? But I didn't get a chance to take in another breath or even figure out the answers before Kade sauntered in.

Dark circles marred the undersides of his eyes. His hair was disheveled as though he'd been through a wind tunnel, and a frown made him look distraught, as though he were fighting a war I wasn't aware of.

I motioned to sit up.

He rushed to my side and pressed a button on the bed.

Once my upper body was elevated and I could see the room more clearly, I asked, "What's wrong? You look like you've been beat up."

He grasped my hand. "You scared the fuck out of me. That's all. What did the nurse say? She kind of looked at me weird when she walked out of the room."

Do I tell him or not? Do I even go down that road to get his hopes up before my test results come back?

"I'm sorry I scared you."

He kissed the back of my hand. "It's not your fault. And I'm good."

I narrowed my gaze. "Liar."

He traced circles on my hand. "That day in high school came screaming back when you passed out on the mound."

"It's not my PTSD."

"I know," he said. "You've been under a lot of stress. And I'm part of it."

"You?"

"Maybe I'm stressing you out being on the road with you."

I rolled my eyes. "Seriously, Kade Maxwell. I love that you're with me. It's just... you're right. Too much is going on, and I'm trying to make sure I play as well or better than any guy on my team. I've been a little paranoid lately about the Sea Dogs not signing me next year."

"Tara said they don't want to lose you."

I nodded. "I know. But I have nothing in writing other than my current contract."

"Lace, your health comes first."

And so does the baby's, I wanted to say.

I gnawed on my lip. *Oh God. A baby.* Parts of me were scared, overwhelmed, excited, apprehensive, confused, and so many other things. Considering I didn't exactly keep track of my periods, I was curious how far along I would be if I were pregnant. Kade and I had been having sex frequently. During All-Star break, we'd been inseparable, and since he'd been on the road with me, we had sex just about every night.

"What's wrong?" Kade asked, knowing full well I had something on my mind.

I inhaled through my nose. "Who was on the phone?" No way was I telling him I could be carrying our baby. One, I wasn't ready to say that out loud. And two, I couldn't get his hopes up only to have them squashed if the test results were negative.

Our baby. I turned that over and over in my head, and a twinge of giddiness coursed through me, causing me to smile wide.

"Kody. He and Jessie got a gig this weekend in New York City. So I have to head home to manage the club." He cocked his head. "Why are you smiling all of a sudden?"

"I love you."

He leaned down and kissed me on the lips. "You are my polar bear."

OMG! He hadn't called me that in forever. I slipped my tongue into his mouth, and when I did, he took control of the kiss.

We stayed glued to one another until a man cleared his throat.

The gray-haired man in scrubs waltzed up to the other side of my bed. "Lacey Maxwell." He held out his hand. "I'm Dr. Johnson. My youngest daughter is in awe of you." He took out a notepad and pen. "Can I get your autograph for her?"

Kade straightened, grinning.

I took the pad and pen. "Sure. What's your daughter's name?"

"Crystal."

I wrote her name then scribbled my usual words. "Dare to Dream." Then I signed my name and drew a heart.

After I handed it back to him, he glanced at Kade then me. "You seem to be doing better. But I'm going to listen to your heart and lungs." He removed the stethoscope from around his neck. "We put a rush on your blood sample. So we should have the results within the hour."

When he was done with his normal checks, he tapped some keys on the computer. "So far, everything seems normal, and your blood pressure has returned to normal. I suspect you were severely dehydrated. You need to get more fluids in your body." He spoke in an even tone.

As an athlete and a healthy person, I knew that. "I've been drinking Gatorade and water."

"What else can cause her to pass out like that?" Kade asked.

"A host of other things. Heart problems can affect blood pressure, diet, and possibly pregnancy." Dr. Johnson glanced at me. "Could you be pregnant?"

I held my breath, peeking at Kade.

His mouth was hanging down to the bed. "Pregnant?" Kade set his copper gaze on me. "Are you? You were puking this morning."

I shrugged. I didn't feel pregnant. "I told you I was throwing up because of the food I ate for dinner."

"Let's wait for the blood test before we get ahead of things," Dr. Johnson said.

I snorted. Easier said than done when it came to my gorgeous husband and me being pregnant. I could see the wheels turning in Kade's head, and that goofy grin he was sporting was telling me he was ready to scream for joy.

In that moment, his tempered happiness was starting to rub off on me. Crap, if he was that happy, I wanted to see him like that more often. Kade was a reserved guy. He held in his feelings in public unless he was pissed off at someone. Still, he hardly wore his feelings on his sleeve. But all bets were off if Dr. Johnson confirmed I was pregnant.

Blaire stuck her head in and handed a piece of paper to Dr. Johnson. "Lacey's blood results."

Kade grasped my hand.

I held my breath.

Dr. Johnson scanned the sheet of paper before turning to Kade and me.

Kade's hold on my hand grew tighter.

Dr. Johnson smiled. "Congratulations. You're going to be parents."

"I'm sorry," Kade said. "Can you repeat that?"

I playfully swatted him. "We're going to have a baby." My tone was light and free even though a part of me was nervous as hell.

The color drained from Kade's face, although he'd had a few minutes to take in the possibility that I could be pregnant before the nurse came in with the results. Despite that, he hadn't lost his goofy grin. "You're serious? Lacey is pregnant?"

Dr. Johnson nodded. "Blood tests usually don't lie," he said in a playful tone.

"But she's on contraception," Kade added, still not onboard with believing all this.

"Contraception isn't a hundred percent foolproof," I said as though I were the doctor.

Kade let go of my hand and stepped back from the bed, shoving his fingers through his hair.

For a split second, anxiety settled in my chest, making my heart beat erratically. He wanted a kid. He was desperate to start a family, but he wasn't giving me a warm and fuzzy feeling. And I'd thought I would be the one to snap.

CHAPTER 13
KADE

Holy fuck! We're going to have a baby.

I started pacing in short strides next to Lacey's bed. I wanted to scream to the world that we were pregnant, but something deep in my gut told me not to get ahead of myself. Maybe because Lacey wasn't freaking out like I thought she would. Or maybe because all this was happening too fast.

Dad had always told us boys, *"Make sure you have all the facts before you react."*

"Just to be real sure, I have to hear you say it again, Dr. Johnson." Maybe hearing his great fucking news for a third time would make it stick like glue.

"You're going to be a father, Mr. Maxwell."

My heart exploded. Hearing him say I was about to be a father was surreal, scary, and exhilarating.

Father. I'm going to be a father. I need to tell the world. I need to call my parents. I can't wait to see Mom's face when I tell her. Hell, my old man is going to be just as stoked.

I stopped wearing a hole in the floor and eyed Lacey.

Tears floated in her eyes as she nodded once.

Suddenly, I wanted to cry with her. But crying wasn't part of my MO.

"I'll give you two a minute," Dr. Johnson said before he left the room.

When we were alone, silence stretched between us as we stared at one another.

A lone tear escaped Lacey's eye and trickled down her rosy cheek. "Come here." She held out her hand.

An electric charge zinged up my arm the minute my fingers closed over hers. As if her touch was enough to open my vault of emotions, tears shot out. "So it's true?"

She giggled through a sniffle. "You heard the doc. Blood tests don't lie."

"But what about your IUD?"

She shrugged. "It happens," she said casually, as though a baby growing inside her was no big deal.

I blinked a few times to dry my own tears. "And you're not disappointed?"

Snap out of it, man. Your wife is happy. She's glowing. Look at her.

"I'm not going to lie. I'm nervous as hell. I'm also happy and shocked. But disappointed? No. I want kids."

"What about baseball?"

She sighed heavily. "Tara said a pregnancy wouldn't end my career, and I have to trust her. Now we'll see if the Sea Dogs live up to their words."

Lacey wanted to believe the Sea Dogs would support her when she got pregnant, but she had her doubts.

"You're going to be a dad, Kade Maxwell." Her tone was giddy. "And a great one too."

I grinned as my nerves spun a web inside me. I liked the sound of Dad. But my gut was telling me not to get too excited. I didn't know why. Maybe because I had a slew of questions that I couldn't answer.

Would I be a good dad? Would my kid be healthy? Would it be a boy or a girl? Would Lacey have a tough pregnancy?

I lifted her hand up to my lips. "And you'll be a fantastic mom."

She gave me a ball-busting smile as the weight of the world seemed to whoosh out of her. Then in a flash, her smile was gone. In its place was a look I couldn't quite figure out.

I kissed the backs of her fingers. "What are you thinking about?"

She shuddered a breath. "You may not believe me, but I'm tired, Kade. I'm tired of worrying about baseball, you, me, us, and our family. I'm tired of putting in a hundred and ten percent effort. I'm tired of not seeing you for months on end. Sometimes I feel like I put in all this effort and I'm getting nowhere."

I lowered her hand to the bed then leaned over and brushed my lips over hers. "You've come a long way, Lacey." I pecked her on the lips. "You've done something that not many or any woman has in your career." I kissed her nose. "You're not quitting baseball. No matter if the Sea Dogs sign you again or not." I kissed her cheek. "You're a fighter." I kissed her other cheek. "You're my baseball beauty, and having a child will not hurt your career at all."

She threw her arms around my neck. "I love the crap out of you." Then her lips connected with mine.

I dove in and kissed her lights out. This woman was my world, my life, my heart, and my soul. Whatever fate had in store for us, we would persevere. We always did.

I tugged her bottom lip as I broke the kiss. "You're going to be even more beautiful pregnant." At that thought, Mr. Steel came alive.

"And you're going to be relentless, making sure you dote on me every day."

I moved stray hairs off her face. "Fuck yeah."

"So what now?" she asked.

"You have a season to finish. Although I am concerned you might pass out again."

"I'm not obligated to tell the team I'm pregnant, but they do need to know," she said. "I'll make sure I eat right and stay hydrated."

I gave her a cheeky grin. "I'm going to be a dad. My mom is going to go nuts."

The color drained from her. "Call me superstitious, but let's not say anything just yet. I want to find out how far along I am, and I want to make sure nothing jinxes this."

I wasn't sure I could contain my excitement. My parents knew me too well, and they would know I was keeping some big news from them. "I'll try."

"Kade Maxwell, you can't even tell your brothers. And I suggest we wait until I have my first ultrasound."

She had a point about jinxes. I couldn't get Mom's hopes up only to shatter them if something did happen or if the blood results were a false positive.

Wait! False positive?

"What's wrong?" Lacey asked. "You look like you've seen a ghost."

I remembered Mom sharing with me how her pregnancy test had been a false positive when she and Dad were trying to conceive before she'd gotten pregnant with my sister. The family had gotten excited only to be let down when she'd found out she wasn't pregnant.

"What if the media gets ahold of the news? If you tell the team, it's going to leak out."

She sucked in her bottom lip. "True. I'll hold off then on telling the team too. I only have a month left of the season anyway."

I was going to be a dad. Lacey was going to be a mom.

In that moment, I couldn't ask for anything else.

CHAPTER 14
LACEY

The last month of the season had dragged by. I'd been plagued with morning sickness every darn day. I felt as though I might puke up the baby at times. Different smells affected me too. I couldn't stand the aroma of coffee, and for some reason, I wanted to puke for hours when Kade drank his coffee in the morning. Other scents like pizza made me hurl, and I loved pizza.

The good news was that by the time I'd shown up for the games, the morning sickness was gone. But I didn't need to worry about the games anymore since the season had ended a week ago.

I sat on the exam table, waiting for the doctor to come in.

Kade paced the room. He'd been anxious since he found out the great news. I knew he was trying not to spill his guts to his parents. We'd had dinner with them last Sunday, and his mom had kept asking him what was wrong.

Kade's response had been, "Just a lot on my mind with the club."

His answer wasn't exactly a lie. The club had been plagued with two robberies in the last month. At first, Kade had thought Marcus was the culprit, but Marcus had sworn it wasn't him. Kade hadn't believed him and, to this day, still didn't. Marcus was turning out to be quite the rebellious kid in the family. But that wasn't my concern.

I swung my legs back and forth. "You're going to make yourself sick. Any headaches?"

Kade came to an abrupt stop. "No. But if we don't get this appointment over with, I might just explode." His voice was even, and his features were pinched tight.

"Come here, big guy." I held out my hands.

He lowered his shoulders, sighing. "I'm sorry. There's so much going on, and I'll be better once I see the fetus and once I can share the news with my parents. My mom is worried, and I hate that I'm the one she's worried about."

If I knew his mom, she'd probably figured out that I was pregnant. Women had a way of connecting the dots. Not to mention, I'd hardly eaten when we had dinner with them last week.

I hooked my fingers inside the waist of my husband's jeans. "You know you'll be a nervous wreck until I deliver." Between his excitement and nerves, he probably wouldn't sleep for the next eight months. Hell, he hadn't for the last month.

"I just want everything to be okay with the baby."

"And it will be," I said with loads of confidence. "Are you afraid there isn't a baby growing inside me?" He'd shared with me how his mom had had a false positive on one of her pregnancies.

He kissed my forehead. "Not at all." He cupped my breasts. "These babies tell me you are. They're getting huge." He grinned like an ass.

I poked his hard abs. "Easy. The doctor will be in shortly."

He bent down and kissed each breast.

He was right. My boobs had grown and were painful, as though someone had pumped them with fluid to the point they were about to burst.

"After we have the ultrasound today, I need to tell Tara," I said. "Then the Sea Dogs." With the season over, it was a good time to share the news, especially since I wouldn't be returning for spring training. They needed to know well in advance anyway.

A knock on the door resonated before Dr. Gardner came in wearing his white lab coat over black dress slacks. He was a handsome older man with salt-and-pepper hair. "Are you two ready?"

A blond nurse glided in behind Dr. Gardner and headed straight for the ultrasound machine.

Nodding, Kade stepped away so Dr. Gardner could get started.

After listening to my heart and lungs, Dr. Gardner wrapped his stethoscope around his neck. "Everything sounds fine. Let's check on the baby."

The word "baby" sent a shiver up my spine. I still wasn't used to the idea that I was pregnant. In that moment, I wished my mom and sister were there. I blinked several times so I wouldn't start bawling. Julie and Mom would've been ecstatic if they were alive. Mom would've already had a list of names written out. Julie would've had the baby shower planned.

Kade came over. "Are you okay?"

I bobbed my head. "I will be. I was just thinking of Julie and Mom."

He grasped my hand. "They're here, baby."

"If it's a girl, we're going to name her Julie. Right?" He and I had decided on that at our wedding.

"Of course," he said.

The nurse, Brenda, turned on the ultrasound machine. A beep sounded when she did.

"Lacey," Dr. Gardner said. "We're going to do a transvaginal ultrasound. This will give us a more accurate picture of how far along you are."

Brenda helped me position my feet in the stirrups. Then she handed Dr. Gardner the wand.

"I got it from here," Dr. Gardner said to Brenda.

Without a word, she left the room.

My pulse quickened as Dr. Gardner started the procedure. "We won't be able to determine the sex until your second trimester, and I doubt you're that far along."

Kade and I did want to know the sex of the baby. We wanted to prepare the baby's room and get things ready.

Butterflies took flight as my gaze bounced around from the screen to Dr. Gardner to Kade.

Kade's gaze was glued to the ultrasound machine.

Honestly, I couldn't tell a darn thing on that screen. All I could make out was static and gray matter.

Every now and then, Dr. Gardner pressed a button on the machine.

"So," I said to break the silence and calm my nerves. "How far along am I?"

Dr. Gardner's focus was on the screen. "One second, Lacey."

Maybe there wasn't a baby inside me.

"What's wrong?" Kade asked, his eyebrows knitting together.

I held my breath.

Dr. Gardner pointed at the screen. "Well..." He sighed. "First, you're definitely about three months along by the size of the fetus." He drew an outline on the screen. "See?"

Relief coursed through me as my heart rate went from zero to a hundred. I was pregnant. So that was good news.

"But?" I asked. *Please don't give us bad news.*

I could clearly make out a tiny speck on the screen but honestly couldn't see anything more than that. I squeezed the life out of Kade's hand, or maybe he was the one gripping my hand so hard.

I blew out a breath and eyed Kade. His mouth was open, fear leaping off of him. My chest rose and fell as I tried to stay calm.

Please let everything be okay with the baby.

I'd done a ton of research prior to my visit, and I'd learned that I would be able to hear the baby's heartbeat at eight weeks, and the doctor had just told us I was three months along. So...

"Is there no heartbeat?" I asked. I hadn't heard one yet.

The color drained from Kade's tanned complexion.

Dr. Gardner fiddled with the machine, turning a knob. When he did, the *boom, boom, boom* resonated.

Kade and I sighed together.

OMG! This was real. Before that moment, I'd come to terms with being pregnant. I had all the symptoms, but hearing a heartbeat was... I didn't know how to describe the feeling. It was intense and overwhelming. I couldn't stop the tears.

Suddenly, butterflies fluttered in my stomach like they were having a party in my honor.

"Then what is it?" Kade asked, a deep crease forming in between his brows.

Dr. Gardner set his dark gaze on me then Kade. "Well, you're going to be the proud parents of not one baby but three."

Kade reared back.

I gasped.

Kade's jaw hit the table. "There's three!"

Dr. Gardner nodded then proceeded to show us all three fetuses. "You two are having triplets."

What in the world? "Triplets?"

"They do run in my family," Kade said as a matter of fact, like he'd been expecting us to have three babies at once.

I was happy to be pregnant, but now I was freaking out. "How in the world am I going to carry three babies in my belly?"

Kade chuckled. "My mom did it."

So the heck what? I knew women carried more than one baby. But not me.

"The body is an amazing vessel," Dr. Gardner said. "And you're in great shape. So that bodes well for you too."

I wanted to bop the doctor over the head. Who used the word "vessel" to describe the human body?

As Kade and Dr. Gardner talked, my mind drifted. No more flat stomach. No more toned body. No more anything for a while. Hell, I wouldn't be able to pitch even if I wanted to, not with how big my belly was going to get with three growing humans inside me.

I was thankful baseball season was over.

Dr. Gardner finished the tests then asked us to meet him in his office. Once he was gone and I was on two feet, Kade picked me up and swung me around.

"I thought hearing you were pregnant was good news, but this tops everything."

I hugged him back, relishing his excitement.

When he was done making me a bit dizzy, he asked, "You're not happy?"

Of course he could sense my tension. "I am. But you realize I will be carrying not one, not two, but three babies." I held up three fingers. Oh, if only men could have kids.

"I will be waiting on you hand and foot, Lace. I'll make sure you don't have to lift a thing."

How could I not smile at that or at the way his copper eyes were dancing in delight?

In that moment, I felt like a tool. I shouldn't have been complaining. We were starting our family off with a bang.

"I can't wait to find out the sex," he said with too much giddiness in his voice. "And I can't wait to share the news with the family on Sunday."

If he lasted that long. The man was bursting at the seams to shout to the world that he was going to be a father.

I giggled. "I've never seen you so happy before." At our wedding, he had been on top of the world, but the spark in his eyes was brighter than ever. It was our family—our growing family.

CHAPTER 15
KADE

Oranges and golds colored the landscape around our house. Lacey and I were hosting our first family gathering with all my brothers and their significant others along with my two nieces and my parents.

I stood out on the deck, grilling steaks, watching how the family was happy and talking and relaxed. Man, I loved days like this when we were all together.

Smoke billowed out of the grill as I lifted the lid. The steaks were almost done, and I couldn't wait to sit down at the table and share the good news. Fuck, I'd been dying to spill my guts for well over a month. Anytime I'd seen Mom, I wanted to tell her we were having a kid, especially when she'd asked if anything was bothering me.

My response had been, "There's a lot going on at the club."

We'd had two break-ins, and I would bet money that Marcus had had something to do with them, but he'd sworn up and down that he was nowhere near the club on the nights in question.

For some reason, a part of me believed him. When Kody had found him passed out on the stage and we'd threatened to call the cops, he'd been scared out of his fucking mind.

Still, Christine was close to sending him off to a military school. My dad had suggested the same academy my brothers had gone to after Kody and Kross had beaten Greg Sullivan into a coma. Whether Christine followed through on that or not wasn't any of my business.

My sole focus and worry was Lacey and our three babies.

Shit.

I was having trouble wrapping my mind around three babies. As happy as I was with triplets, part of me was wondering how we would manage three, particularly when Lacey returned to playing ball.

I shouldn't worry. Mom was a stone's throw from our house, and my aunt Christine was a few miles down the road. I was sure they had some great advice, especially Mom, who'd raised triplets.

Speaking of my brothers, Kelton waltzed out from the kitchen with his signature cocky grin plastered on his unshaven jaw. His blue eyes glistened in the afternoon sun. "Those steaks ready yet?"

I flipped the steaks over. "Nope. Too lazy to shave this weekend?" I teased.

He arched a brow. "You must be lazy too." He circled his finger in the air around my face.

"Touché."

We both chuckled.

Kelton scrutinized me as though I were on the witness stand. "You look different since the last time I saw you."

It figured he could see right through me. He was officially a lawyer, albeit a freshman lawyer. He'd just about aced the bar exam and was working for a prestigious law firm in Boston.

"What's going on?" he asked. "Getting laid more, I suspect, now that baseball season is over."

Leave it to Kelton to always fit sex into the conversation.

I grinned as my gaze drifted past my brother and landed on Lacey, who was talking to my mom. She had her hair up in a messy bun. Her cheeks were pink and not from makeup. Her breasts... Well, those babies were growing at the speed of light, and with her slim, toned body, it was hard not to notice how big her tits were.

I mentally shook off any images of her naked. Kelton wasn't wrong in the least. I couldn't get enough of my gorgeous wife.

My mom reared back as she listened to Lacey. For a split second, my stomach did a somersault, wondering if my wife was spilling the beans to Mom before dinner. But as soon as that thought hit me, I chucked it. Lacey wanted me to tell my family. She was probably telling Mom something about baseball. We'd learned from Tara that another up-and-coming female was making news in the baseball arena, and Lacey was excited to meet her at some point.

Kelton snapped his fingers. "Dude, where did you go?"

I blinked. "Can I look at my wife?"

He narrowed his eyes. "Sure, but..." He studied me more.

I turned to check on the steaks, hoping he didn't probe any further. I wasn't sure I could contain myself. I'd been bursting to tell someone. I hadn't even told my best bud, Hunter, and I told him everything. Sure, I shared a ton with my brothers, but I was afraid Kross would tell his wife Ruby, and Ruby couldn't keep a secret to save her life. At least according to Kross she couldn't.

Kelton's girl, Lizzie, wanted kids so bad that I couldn't imagine her keeping anything to herself. As far as Jessie, Kody's girl, she was probably the only one I did trust with our news. After all, she worked as a nurse and was accustomed to keeping patient news to herself.

Despite all that, I wanted to see everyone's face at one time when I told them we were having triplets.

"You're hiding something." Kelton's voice drew me back to him.

I schooled my features into what I hoped was one of my blank expressions that Lacey despised.

"I know you, dude. I can see it in the way you're holding in a fucking grin that I'm sure is the size of Massachusetts." Then he regarded Lacey and swung his gaze back to me. "Holy shit!"

The fucker was putting the puzzle pieces together. I shouldn't have been surprised. Kelton's lawyer instincts in reading people were killer. The man could read the life of a stranger walking on the street. At times, I thought he had clairvoyant skills.

Smoke floated out and around the grill.

"Whatever it is you think you know, shut it," I said in a harsh tone.

He leaned in close to me as I mindlessly poked the steaks with a fork. "When is she due?" His voice was barely audible.

Reaghan, my two-year-old niece, ran out with Kross chasing his daughter. Her black-as-night curls bounced with every step she took as she squealed.

"Daddy's going to get you," Kross said as Reaghan latched on to my leg.

"Uncle Kade," she cooed, her tiny hands digging into my leg.

I handed the fork to Kelton. "Can you pile the steaks on the plate?" Then I lifted Reaghan up and into my arms. "Hey, button. I'll protect you from the big bad wolf."

She giggled as her tiny hand latched on to my neck. "Daddy's not a wolf, silly."

Kross bared his teeth in an attempt to mimic a wolf with long fangs. "I'm coming to get my little Red Riding Hood." His blue eyes went wide.

According to Kross, Reaghan loved when he read *Little Red Riding Hood* to her at bedtime.

She stuck out her little chin and flashed those big blue eyes at her dad. "I'm not afraid of the big bad wolf."

Kelton, Kross, and I burst out laughing. The child would be a force to contend with, as she got older. I couldn't help but think about the triplets we were having.

Holy fuck! Every time I thought about three babies, I had to pinch myself. Regardless, I wanted my kids to be strong and not take shit from anyone.

Kross grabbed Reaghan from me. "Something is off with you, bro."

Reaghan rested her head on Kross's shoulder.

Kelton piled the steaks on a platter, chuckling.

I rolled my eyes. "I'm good." *Better than good.* But we needed to get the food on the table and everyone seated. Otherwise, I was going to burst.

Reaghan lifted her head, planting her hand on Kross's cheek. "I'm hungry."

"Me too, sweetie," Kross said. "Well, bro. What is it? Lacey and baseball? Did she get any more offers from Triple-A teams?"

Kelton carried the plate of steaks into the house, shaking his head before he announced loudly, "Time to eat."

I sighed in relief and silently thanked Kelton for the distraction. Everyone scattered, as though they were starving, except Lacey, who glided toward me.

Kross carried his daughter inside without waiting for an answer to his question, which was fine with me. Baseball wasn't on my mind. However, Tara was talking to the Sea Dogs about Lacey's contract.

After Lacey had shared our good news with Tara, and Tara had come down from her excitement, she'd told Lacey she would talk with the Sea Dogs's management on Lacey's behalf.

Lacey winked at Reaghan and maybe Kross as they breezed by her.

Sounds of voices faded as the family settled in the dining room, leaving Lacey and me alone in the kitchen.

She lifted up on her tiptoes. "You ready?" She beamed like a bright light shining through the fog on a humid night.

I inhaled her citrus scent as I wrapped my arms around her. "More than ready." Then I kissed her—slow, wet, and teasingly long for good measure.

She let out a whisper of a moan. "We better get in there before I drag you into the bedroom."

I started thinking of sports and cars and anything else to get rid of the bulge in my jeans. My dick was throbbing and itching to get out and inside my sexy wife.

"Go," I said to Lacey. "I need a minute."

Her gaze latched on to my groin, and she giggled. "Don't be too long." She pivoted on her heel and wiggled her ass teasingly.

"Lace," I warned.

She tossed one of her *come fuck me* looks as she licked her lips.

"You'll pay for this later."

"I know."

Once I was alone, I took in a few deep breaths, adjusting my dick. Then I shook my head and joined the family.

Eleven pairs of eyes looked up as I walked in.

I found a spot behind Lacey at the head of the table and gripped the back of her chair. She pushed to her feet and came around to hold my hand.

Mom flashed her blue eyes wide as though she knew what we were about to say.

I blinked once, and Lacey squeezed my hand as if to say, "You got this."

I swung my gaze around the room, stopping to look at each person for a brief second. The only one relaxing back in his chair was Kelton. He was watching and waiting to see the reactions on everyone's faces.

Lizzie, Kelton's girl, flipped her black hair over her shoulder before she angled her head toward Lacey and me. Ruby had a crease in between her bluish-green eyes.

"Why are you standing up, Uncle Kade?" Raven asked.

Kross kissed his eight-year-old daughter on the side of her head, moving her braid off her shoulder. "I think he and Aunt Lacey have some big news to tell us."

Mom's expression perked up.

Jessie and Kody, who were the closest to Lacey and me, sat quietly.

I draped my arm around Lacey and tugged her to me. Then I regarded my parents. "Lacey and I are having a baby." A sigh poured out of me, taking with it all the pent-up tension from keeping that secret for over a month.

Tears filled Mom's blue eyes. The women squealed, as did Raven and her sister, Reaghan, although Reaghan probably didn't get the full meaning of what I'd just said.

Dad came over to give me a hug. "I'm so happy for you." Then he wrapped his arms around Lacey.

Before I knew what was happening, my brothers got in line to congratulate us. Then Lizzie, Ruby, and Jessie followed suit. My nieces stayed at the table, munching on bread rolls. The last to hug me was Mom.

Her hug was tight as happy tears flowed down her beautiful skin. "I had an inkling something was up." She regarded Lacey. "I can see a physical change in you."

Her tits for sure.

She held out her arm to Lacey. "Come here."

Lacey stepped into Mom's arms as she prodded me with her eyes to tell them the rest.

"So when are you due?" Mom asked Lacey.

The low chatter that had ensued quickly died.

"Well..." I said.

Everyone was listening intently except the kids.

"Lacey will be delivering triplets in April."

With the exception of my nieces, everyone's jaws hit the wooden table. Mom, who was sandwiched in between Lacey and me, swayed a little before she threw her arms around me once again.

"Holy cow!" Kody said. "Way to go, bro."

Mom released me then hugged Lacey.

I looked at my dad. He nodded as if to say, "You got this. You were born to raise triplets."

In a way, I guess I was. I'd taken care of my brothers after Karen had died when my mom was living in a mental health facility for a couple of years.

"Do you know what the sex is?" Lizzie asked.

"How far along are you?" Ruby asked.

"You know, we should start planning the baby shower," Mom added.

The buzz and excitement filling the room was making me a bit dizzy.

Mom returned to her seat next to Dad.

"Your mom and I are so proud of you, Kade," Dad said. "We're proud of all of you." Dad regarded my brothers. "You've grown into responsible young men who know what family means."

Tears threatened as I took in a deep breath. "You've raised us right."

Kelton, Kross, and Kody chimed in with the same, nodding their heads.

Jessie, Kody's girl, finally spoke up. "So, triplets! I'm so happy for you two." She set her loving expression on Kody.

"One day, baby doll," Kody said to Jessie as though he knew what her expression meant.

Kody hadn't proposed to her yet. For that matter, Kelton hadn't proposed to Lizzie yet either. Both had their reasons.

"Lacey," Lizzie said, tucking strands of her black hair behind her ear. "Are you ready to carry three babies?"

Ruby joined the conversation as she filled Reaghan and Raven's plates with food. "Carrying one is enough."

Lacey and I took our seats. She was at one end of the table, and I was at the other.

Kody handed Lacey a bowl of potato salad. "Honestly, I'm a little scared."

Mom reached over and patted Lacey's hand. "I'll be here for you. It's not as daunting as it sounds. The body is amazing."

Jessie buttered a roll. "She's right. You might have to be on bed rest or at least off your feet toward the end, but as long as you stay in shape, triplets will be a breeze for you," the nurse in her said.

I exchanged a thankful look with my dad, blinking and nodding at him as I swallowed down a ton of emotions waiting to burst free, from love to trepidation and everything in between. But I was more than ready to start down this road. I was more than ready to tend to screaming babies at three in the morning. I was more than ready to expand my family. And I was definitely more than ready to do all of that with the woman who'd stolen my heart seven years ago in the high school parking lot.

CHAPTER 16
LACEY

My eyes flew open as a gripping pain had me trying to catch my breath. I sat up and checked the time. The clock on the nightstand was flashing four a.m. I swung my gaze over to Kade, who was fast asleep, which was unlike him. He'd been tossing and turning just about every night for the last two months of my pregnancy.

I'd gotten so big that I couldn't do much. I couldn't even see my ankles when I stood. I was so ready to have these babies. The kicking and heartburn and peeing and pain in my lower back were getting to be too much.

I climbed out of bed, or more like waddled out, pushing off the mattress to stand upright, my belly protruding out over my feet.

Argh! I was so ready to see my ankles. I was so ready to get back to my normal body. I often wondered how I would've even pitched if I'd been playing. Standing on the mound with my belly growing, trying to cock my leg and release the ball would've not only been impossible but comical. My belly had started to poke out at four months. Then at five, with three babies inside me, I blew up like a darn balloon.

The minute I was standing, a gush of water slid down my thighs followed by a sharp pain in my belly. I bit down on my tongue and counted to three, blowing in and out as I'd done many times during birthing classes when being taught how to handle contractions.

This is it. Time to bring our babies into this world.

Holy crap on a cracker! I held my stomach as pain so sharp kept me from moving.

Breathe. Breathe. Breathe.

I inhaled then exhaled, once, twice, three times.

When the contraction finally subsided, I let out the air in my lungs. I wasn't sure if I was ready for more pain to come.

Nevertheless, I went over to Kade's side of the bed. He looked peaceful, and I hated to wake him. The man had bags under his eyes and needed more rest than me, with as much running around and doting on me as he'd done.

I dragged a nail down his arm lightly. "Kade, honey."

His eyes moved rapidly behind his lids.

Crap. REM sleep. That meant he was deep into this sleep cycle.

Before I freaked out too much or another pain gripped me, I went into our en suite bathroom and cleaned up. Then I changed out of my sleep shirt and into a pair of yoga pants and an oversized T-shirt. Then I grabbed my hospital bag, which we had prepared a month ago, and deposited it at the door.

I ambled back to my sleeping giant. "Hey, baby," I said in a louder voice than before, shaking him.

As I did, a contraction made me moan, and I clutched his arm so hard, I dug my nails into him.

His eyes shot open. He blinked rapidly, looking out of sorts. "What's wrong?"

I took in several short breaths, puffing them out, closing my eyes, and trying to stay on my feet when all I wanted to do was keel over and curl up into a fetal position.

Kade flew off the bed then helped me sit down. "It's time. Isn't it?" His voice cracked.

I nodded as the contraction waned. "We need to get moving. My water broke, and I think the babies are coming fast."

The ladies in my birthing class who were on their second pregnancies had said their first deliveries took hours because they were in labor for so long.

Something told me the three inside me weren't going to take hours.

He spun around, running his hand through his hair, searching the room. "Oh shit. Where the fuck are my clothes?"

I giggled for no other reason than to calm myself down.

He whipped his tired eyes at me. "Seriously? You're laughing at me?"

I shook my head. "No. I just envisioned how this night would go, and never in a million years did I think you would freak out."

Once he found his jeans, he stumbled as he managed to get one leg in then the other. "Bag?"

I stabbed a finger at the door as I rose, pushing out my stomach to balance myself. I giggled again. Between my breasts and my belly, which was as big as the universe, I was surprised I didn't fall forward. I wobbled when I was on two feet.

Flinging the bag over his shoulder, Kade rushed over to me then wrapped his fingers around my arm. "Okay, let's go."

"I can walk. I'm not ninety years old," I teased. "Besides, you need a shirt. Unless you want the nurses drooling over you."

He reared back. "Fuck." He let go of me, dropping the bag as he practically vaulted in the air toward his dresser.

I waddled as I headed to the door. I might as well get a head start.

Kade pulled out the first T-shirt his hands landed on and shrugged into it as though he were the Flash. Once he was fully dressed, with the bag over his shoulder, I was in the hallway.

"How far along are the contractions?" he asked.

"No idea." I should have been counting, but I'd been too busy getting ready. "All I know is the pain seems to be coming faster and faster."

When we reached the kitchen, I let out a moan that sounded like someone was stabbing me.

"Breathe," he said.

I snarled. "I'm trying. Get the car," I said through clenched teeth.

"Lace, you need to breathe."

My nostrils flared. "Please, get the car. I'll meet you out front."

He studied me for a beat, his eyebrows drawing down, debating if he should leave me. "Fuck no. I'm not leaving you." He paled.

I held on to the wall outside the kitchen. "By the time you"—I moaned as the pain seemed to intensify—"get the car, the pain"—I inhaled then exhaled—"will be gone."

He didn't move.

I planted my hand on his heart, which was beating out of his chest. "I know you want to make sure I'm okay. But if you don't get the car, I'm going to have these babies on our kitchen floor."

He mashed his lips into a thin line then bolted down the hall toward the garage.

I loved the attention. I loved being home with him. I loved that he took care of me. But I was ready to be my own person again. I felt like I'd been cooped up and unable to breathe at times. And if I were being honest, I was missing baseball. The season had started, and I wasn't there. But the season and playing ball would have to wait.

The contraction finally started to subside. Then as fast as I could go, I met Kade in the driveway.

He rushed around to the passenger's side and helped me in. Then like a madman, he got behind the wheel. He sped through the quiet streets of Ashford. The ten-minute ride to the hospital was quiet except for my moans when a contraction came barreling down on me once again.

When he screeched to a halt under the portico to the emergency room, Kade threw the car in Park and jumped out.

An orderly was outside with a wheelchair in hand as though he were waiting for us. He'd probably seen Kade's erratic driving as we sped into the hospital lot.

"My wife is in labor," Kade all but shouted.

As calm as the ocean on a windless day, the orderly smiled. "Park your car, sir. I'll take the missus inside."

Kade's forehead creased. "Are you mad? She's in labor, and I'm not leaving her."

I eased down into the wheelchair. "Park the car, honey. I'll be fine."

He muttered swear words under his breath as he sped off once again.

"Thank you," I said to the orderly, whose name on his uniform read Fred.

"I see this all the time," Fred said, wheeling me in. "So, contractions close?"

I'd had another contraction halfway to the hospital. If I was counting correctly, they were about five or six minutes apart. "They are."

"Well then, I'll get you up to maternity in two shakes of a lamb's tail." He did as promised, rolling me into the maternity ward two minutes later. Nurses scrambled when they saw me, as though I were the life of the party, and one of those nurses was my BFF, Becca.

Becca rushed up to me, her dark eyes lighting up. "It's time?"

I nodded. The babies were definitely coming.

"Let's get Lacey prepped and call Dr. Livingston," Becca ordered as though she were in charge of the nurses.

I wanted to ask what she was doing in the maternity ward since she worked in the NICU, but another contraction bore down. "I suddenly feel like I need to push." I winced as the pain blinded me. Thank God I was in a wheelchair. Otherwise, I would be barreled over.

A brunette nurse ran around the nurses' station, and within seconds, the paging system blared, "Dr. Livingston, please report to the maternity ward."

"Her husband is parking the car," Fred said.

Becca replaced Fred behind my wheelchair. "Thanks, Fred. We got this from here. Can you let her husband know where she is?" Then she wheeled me down the hallway. "Kade must be freaking out."

"I thought you worked in NICU," I said in between breathing like I'd been running for miles.

"I'm filling in for someone tonight. Don't worry—you're in good hands. And since you're having triplets, you'll have a team of nurses in the delivery room."

I wasn't worried. I was sure Becca was great at her job. "I'm so glad you're here. But you mentioned Dr. Livingston. Can you call Dr. Gardner?" I knew I might not get him, depending on whether he was on call, but I sure was going to try.

"We will, but Dr. Livingston is on duty tonight. And she's great."

I'd only met Dr. Livingston once, and as the pain took hold, I guessed it didn't matter which doctor delivered the babies, as long as I got them out of me.

I scrunched up my face. "I need to push again."

She wheeled me into the delivery room as the brunette nurse joined us. "You can't push yet."

Easier said than done.

Sweat beaded on my forehead. The need to push was so strong, I wasn't sure I could abstain.

"Lacey, I'm Jill," the brunette said. "I want you to take in a deep breath and blow it out."

I did as she instructed while they helped me up and onto the bed. As I kept inhaling and exhaling, Becca and Jill managed to undress me before hooking me up to a monitor. The need to push was dire, and I felt like I was about to pass out if I held back any longer. So I shook my head in an effort to distract myself, when Dr. Livingston breezed in.

"How far apart are the contractions?" Dr. Livingston asked as she settled at the foot of the bed.

"Three or four minutes," Becca said as a scurry of activity started to take place around me.

"Hi, Lacey. Nice to see you again." Dr. Livingston smiled warmly, regarding me with kind blue eyes. "Is your husband here?"

The minute she asked, Kade blew through the door like a gust of wind, seeking me out and rushing to my side. Sweat coated his face, his hair was tucked under a blue cap, he was wearing a blue gown over his clothes, and he was breathing hard, as though he'd just run a marathon.

Dr. Livingston nodded her dark head of hair at Kade then addressed us both. "Here's how this will go. I'm going to do a quick exam to see how dilated you are. If you're ready, then we'll get started."

Kade gripped my hand, bobbing his head as he regarded me with panic steeped in his eyes.

"Seriously, you're not going to faint or anything. Are you?" I asked as another contraction hit me. I sucked in a sharp breath as my face contorted. The need to push was stronger than ever.

"Breathe," Kade said in a soft voice.

Becca scrambled to get my feet in the stirrups. Dr. Livingston went to work quickly, examining me.

Kade swiped his hand over my head. "Lace, you're turning red. You have to breathe."

I growled at my husband. "Want to switch places?" Oh, how nice it would be if he could give birth or experience the pain that I was going through.

I finally inhaled, but that did nothing to ease the pain.

"Lacey," Dr. Livingston said. "When I tell you to push, I want you to push as hard as you can. Okay?"

Nodding, I wanted to scream "hell yeah," but I couldn't find my voice as I was trying to get more air in my lungs.

Becca returned to my side.

"Okay, Lacey." Dr. Livingston eyed the monitor near me. "I want you to push now."

Becca placed her hand on my back guiding my upper body forward. "Bear down as hard as you can."

I put every ounce of energy I had into pushing as hard as I could.

"She's turning beet red again." Kade's voice trickled in my ears over my loud grunting. "She's going to pass out."

"You're doing great," Dr. Livingston informed me while the medical staff ignored Kade.

I was sure I was red, but at the moment, I didn't care about anything other than getting the babies out of me.

CHAPTER 17
KADE

My heart was beating out of my chest as Lacey grunted, growled, and groaned.

Over the last few months, I couldn't wait for this moment. I couldn't wait to see Lacey giving birth to our babies. But as I stood next to my wife, who was beet red, in pain, and looked as though she were about to pass out, all I wanted to do was comfort her.

We'd learned what to expect in the delivery room. I'd read books on giving birth. Lacey and I had both tried to be as prepared as possible. But honestly, I couldn't remember a fucking thing I'd read or learned. All I knew was that I wanted to take away Lacey's pain. If I could, I would switch places with her in a heartbeat. I would gladly take on the burden of giving birth if I could.

I hated feeling helpless. So I moved her hair off her sweaty forehead in an attempt to soothe her.

But she growled then swatted at me. "Don't touch me."

My eyebrows shot into my hairline.

Becca shrugged like my wife's reaction was no big deal. "It's normal."

Fuck if it was normal in my world.

"Maybe you should watch the babies being born," Becca said. "I got Lacey."

Granted, Becca had always been there for Lacey in tough times, but I didn't want her to have Lacey. I wanted to be the one to help my wife.

"Don't you want to see them come out?" Lacey asked through clenched teeth.

I had planned to watch the entire process, but I didn't want to leave Lacey's side.

"I see the head of one," Dr. Livingston said. "I want you to bear down as hard as you can, Lacey, and push now."

Lacey took in a deep breath and grunted so loud that the entire hospital had to have heard her.

A chill skated up my spine as anticipation took hold of me like a vise. My heart was still ramming against my ribs. I swore when all this was over, I would have bruised or cracked ribs.

Holding my breath, I watched in quiet fascination as my wife put every ounce of her energy into delivering baby number one.

Before I knew what was happening, a baby cried as Lacey flopped backward, out of breath and looking completely exhausted.

Fuck. She still had two more to deliver, which was the main reason I was going into freak-out mode. Something told me she wouldn't make it through baby number two.

One of the nurses took the baby over to a counter.

Becca wiped a wet cloth over Lacey's forehead and face.

I smiled at my wife as she tried to regulate her breathing. I was just about to say "you're doing great" or something to soothe her when she moaned.

"More contractions," she said in a cracked and tired voice.

Sweat began to bead on my neck. I didn't think I could watch her go through another round of pain. This whole process was gutting me.

As if Dr. Livingston could read my mind, she said, "Kade, stand next to me. You should see your babies being born."

Another nurse who was waiting idly came to my side. "Go. I'll take over from here."

Maybe it was best I didn't help Lacey. Then again, I hadn't been much help so far. I should let the medical professionals do their job anyway.

My phone vibrated in my pocket. I'd left my parents a message that Lacey was in labor. I was sure either Mom or Dad was trying to get ahold of me, but I didn't want to miss baby number two being born.

Dr. Livingston examined Lacey.

Becca gave Lacey some water.

The brunette nurse who had taken my spot stared at the monitor.

I didn't know how much time to expect in between births. We'd learned that with vaginal delivery, it could be minutes or hours before baby number two and three were born. But with the pain on Lacey's face, I didn't think she would be in labor for very long.

"The contractions are intensifying," Lacey said.

"I see baby number two," Dr. Livingston added. "I want you to push, Lacey."

Lacey bent forward, squeezing her eyes shut, scrunching her nose, and grunting loudly.

I stood slightly behind Dr. Livingston so as not to get in her way. From where I was, I had a decent view, but at the moment, all I could see was nothing. Dr. Livingston had her hands inside Lacey.

Lacey let out a scream of all screams as she pushed, and then before I knew what was happening, baby number two was in Dr. Livingston's hands.

Chills blanketed my body.

Holy fuck!

Seeing things from this angle certainly made my pulse race for the finish line. But nothing hit me harder than the sudden realization that I was a father.

Me, Kade Maxwell, was a father. It was at that moment that the light bulb brightened. This shit was real.

I'd had plenty of time to wrap my head around becoming a father and to figure out what I would do when my babies came into this world. All that suddenly went out the window because as I saw the tiny newborn with dark hair, my knees became weak. The room began to spin.

I blinked several times as the sounds around me faded to a distant hum. I listed to one side. I heard someone say something but couldn't make out her words. I shook my head hard when a cold hand landed on my arm.

"You need to sit down, Mr. Maxwell," one of the nurses said.

I swallowed an elephant. "I'm good."

"I need to push again," Lacey said in a tired voice. "I don't think I can, though."

My eyes widened as I focused, or tried to, on my wife, who seemed blurry from where I stood.

The nurse left my side and raced back to Lacey.

I blinked again, and Lacey came into better focus.

She was breathing heavily, drenched in sweat, and looking like she needed nine months to recover.

Hunching over, she squeezed her eyes shut as her face glowed red and then pushed.

Suddenly, an overwhelming feeling gripped me, and the room blurred.

The babies, my babies, cried behind me.

I wanted to move. I wanted to turn around to see them, but I was worried if I did, I might pass out.

I took in short breaths and blew them out while the nurses and doctor did their jobs.

When Lacey let out a bloodcurdling scream or grunt or some fucking sound that I felt down in my bones, I swayed too far to the left as the room went dark.

※

Something burned my nostrils as I jolted awake.

"Mr. Maxwell," a female voice said as she tapped my face lightly.

My eyes watered, and I pinched my nose.

The brunette nurse waved a small capsule under my nose. "Are you okay?"

I glanced around. I was still in the delivery room. Dr. Livingston was talking to Lacey. Becca was fiddling with the monitor, and the babies weren't anywhere in sight.

I pushed to my feet, swaying in the process. The nurse steadied me.

Becca came over and grabbed my arm. "Everyone is fine," she said as though she knew what I was thinking. "Lacey did great."

I shoved my fingers through my hair. "Where are the babies?"

"They're down in the nursery," Becca said. Then she regarded the brunette. "Jill, can you get Kade some juice?"

Jill scurried out of the room.

I didn't need any juice. I needed to see Lacey.

With Becca's help, I ambled over to Lacey's bedside. She looked spent, as though she'd been through a war. Hell, she had.

"Hey," Lacey said as her eyelids fluttered closed. "Are you good?"

I kissed her on the forehead. "Never better." I hated that I had passed out, but I couldn't have stopped myself even if I'd tried. The dizziness had hit me like a ten-ton brick. I swung my gaze to Dr. Livingston. "So baby number three came out okay?"

"All three are fine," she said with a smile. "Lacey did well. And don't worry about passing out. It happens to a lot of new fathers."

I chuckled. I wasn't worried. I didn't care what anyone thought of me, except Lacey and my family. Then again, I was sure Lacey would have something more to say about me blacking out when she wasn't about to fall asleep.

We'd talked about the delivery. I'd been excited to see the process. I'd been excited to witness every detail of our babies being born. But everything had been too much.

"Get some rest," Dr. Livingston said to Lacey. "The nurses will bring the babies in later." Then she met Becca at the door and whispered something to her before she left.

Lacey grabbed my hand. "You should call your parents. And can you call my dad?"

I nodded as our gazes locked. "I love the crap out of you." In that moment, I couldn't explain the feeling that took hold of my heart. My love for her was suddenly stronger than it had ever been.

She was my idol. She was my savior. She was my everything.

A tear slipped out and slid down my cheek. We were embarking on a new aspect of our lives, and I couldn't have asked for a better, more beautiful person to do that with than my green-eyed baseball beauty who'd stolen my heart the minute I met her.

CHAPTER 18
LACEY

My eyes fluttered open as the faint noise of the heart monitor droned in the background. My body felt like I'd been through the spin cycle a few times. It took me a second to realize where I was and what I'd been through.

Suddenly, I sat up, searching the room. I blinked once, twice, even a third time. When my vision cleared, I spotted Kade sleeping in a chair next to my bed. He had his legs kicked out, hands folded over his chest, and his head hung off to the side, practically touching his shoulder as he slept.

Aside from my sleeping giant, I didn't see my babies. And I was in what looked to be a private room, not the one I'd delivered the triplets in.

I was about to swing my legs over the side, but my legs were weak, and I groaned in the process, deciding that it wasn't a good idea to try to get out of bed.

Kade stirred before he popped to his feet. "You can't get up yet."

"Why not? I gave birth. It isn't like I broke my legs." But they felt like they didn't have any strength in them.

He fluffed my pillow. "You need to rest."

He was right. So I decided not to argue. "Where are the babies? I want to see them." I had this intense need to hold all three of them.

"They're down in the nursery. I'll see if I can get a wheelchair."

As Kade motioned to leave, Becca came in. "You're awake." Her dark eyes sparkled. "Wonderful. I'll have the babies brought up." She left before I could tell her that I wanted to go to the nursery.

"Are they healthy? Are they okay?" I asked.

Kade grinned. "They're perfect."

A warm feeling spread through me. I couldn't believe I had given birth to three babies. I couldn't believe I was a mom.

I studied him. Dark circles ringed his eyes. His hair was disheveled, and he seemed as though he needed to get in bed with me. "I guess I should ask you if you've recovered. You passed out."

Never in a million years would I have thought this strong man who carried the weight of the world on his shoulders would get queasy. "Did watching me give birth make you sick?"

He chuckled as his dimples emerged. "Honestly, it was overwhelming watching everything happening. You scared me. I swear you were a second away from dying."

Rolling my eyes, I grabbed his hand. When I did, an electrical charge zinged up my arm. The man still made my belly flutter even if he looked tired and a bit pale.

He brought my hand to his lips. "You were amazing despite the pain you were in."

The door opened, and Becca wheeled in the first crib followed by two nurses and the other two cribs.

My heart was beating fast and hard. This was it. I was about to see the tiny humans who'd come out of my body. I'd asked Eleanor how she had carried Kelton, Kross, and Kody. Actually, I had asked her a ton of questions about carrying and raising triplets.

She'd been just as nervous as me when she'd found out she was having three boys. But she'd said it had been the best experience of her life. Raising them had been tiring and tough, and she had wanted to pull her hair out at times, but if she had it to do all over again, she wouldn't have changed a thing.

Becca lifted up baby number one. "Are you ready to hold your first little girl? She was born first."

Kade's face lit up like the northern lights.

The other two nurses positioned the cribs side by side next to my bed then left.

All three babies were wrapped in pink blankets with pink hats on their heads. All were sound asleep too. And they all looked absolutely beautiful.

I couldn't hold back the tears. The emotions—love, relief, and trepidation—were too strong to reel in, and I didn't want to hold back anyway. Kade and I had made these three humans, three tiny girls who would be loved and cherished for the rest of their lives.

I peeked at Kade. He had a tear sliding down his face as he left my side to pick up one of our girls. When he did, I cried some more.

Seeing the happiness jumping off him was priceless. That gleam in his copper eyes, the way he cradled her in his arms, the smile that said "I'm a proud father" gave me a chill that would last a lifetime.

He was going to be a fantastic father, and for that, I cried harder as Becca placed our firstborn in my arms.

I blinked several times to dry the tears so I could take in every detail of this tiny human being.

She had a tiny nose and pink lips, and her cheeks were rosy. I ran my finger over her face lightly so I wouldn't wake her.

"Have you decided on names yet?" Becca asked.

She'd been part of a discussion Kade and I had had a few months ago when she was at the house, checking on me.

I regarded Kade, who was riveted to the baby he was cradling. "We have a few picked out, but we're not set on specifics yet."

Kade and I had only decided on one.

He set the baby back in her crib then picked up baby number three.

I wasn't sure how we would tell them apart.

"Which one was born second?" Kade asked Becca, who was doting on baby number two as she leaned over the crib.

"They have little wristbands on, which you can't see since they're wrapped in their blankets, but their information—like weight, size, and time of birth—are on the white printed labels affixed to the each of the cribs," Becca said through a smile as though she was in love with the babies.

I was sure she was. She would definitely be part of their lives.

Kade rocked back and forth as he stared at the baby in his arms. "She's so fucking beautiful. They're all beautiful."

Becca giggled. "I'm so glad I was on duty." She straightened as tears pooled in her eyes. "This experience has been amazing, more so than others since I got to see my BFF give birth."

I held out my hand as I kept a strong hold on my firstborn. "Come here, girl."

Becca sidled up to the other side of the bed opposite the cribs. "I love you." She squeezed my hand.

"Ditto, girl," I said, wanting to bawl my eyes out for some reason. "You will be a big part of their lives."

She swiped a tear off her cheek. "I'm so in love with them. I feel like I gave birth too." She giggled through a sniffle as she eyed Kade. "Oh, I meant to tell you guys. Kade's parents are in the waiting room. I'll go get them."

Kade's mom was going to spoil these girls rotten. Well, Kade might beat her to it. I suspected the entire family would spoil them, just like they had Kross's two girls.

Becca crossed the room. "Oh, and let me know when you've decided on the names. We'll want to get the birth certificates completed." Then she breezed out of the room.

"So who will be Julie?" Kade asked.

I giggled as a light and airy feeling floated in my chest. I felt as though my sister, Julie, were there with us.

I lifted a shoulder as I kissed my baby's head. "I don't know that it matters. Maybe we name the oldest Julie?" My reasoning behind that was simple. We'd picked the name Julie at our wedding. So it seemed appropriate to name the firstborn Julie.

He nodded. "And this one in my arms, I say we name her Jazlyn or maybe Jordan."

We wanted each of the girls' names to start with the letter J. We felt it was a tradition in the Maxwell family since each of the Maxwell brothers' names began with K. With Kross and Ruby, their daughters were Raven and Reaghan. So since we were naming one of our girls Julie, we wanted to keep the Js going.

"We also have Jade, Jillian, and Josie on the list," I said.

Kade set the baby back in her crib then returned to my bedside. "They all look the same. Until they mature a bit, we'll need to keep name tags on them. That's what Mom did with my brothers."

I remembered Eleanor mentioning that. "We can have their names stitched on their beanies." Then again, they wouldn't be wearing beanies all the time.

"Mom had engraved silver bracelets for Kelton, Kross, and Kody until she could tell them apart."

At the mention of his mom, Eleanor practically flew into the room, all smiles, and her blue eyes glimmered. Martin was on her heels.

Eleanor wasted no time in walking over to the cribs.

I smiled at Kade.

He shook his head.

Normally, Eleanor would give her full attention to Kade, but with more grandchildren, he was slowly dropping down on her list. Judging by the grin on his face, he didn't mind in the least.

Martin, a Kade lookalike, hugged his son. "Congratulations."

"Oh my," Eleanor cooed. "They're beautiful."

My girls were more than beautiful if that were possible.

"Did you call my dad?" I asked Kade while Eleanor lifted up one baby.

"He's flying home next week, and he wants you to call him when you can," Kade said.

Dad was a traveling man as of late. He was knee-deep in signing new bands to his record label, so he was constantly in Los Angeles or some big city around the world.

As much as I wanted to see my dad, I had three little ones who needed my attention.

"Who's who?" Martin asked as he joined his wife, ogling one of the girls.

"This one is Julie," I said as I handed Julie to Kade.

He had a permanent grin as he cradled Julie in his arms. "Hey, baby girl."

I placed a hand over my heart, trying to reel in my emotions. Seeing Kade and how happy he was made my heart burst.

"The other two, we're not sure yet," I said as I slumped back in the bed, not taking my eyes off my handsome husband.

My body was tired, my brain was slowly shutting down, and suddenly, I wanted to sleep. "But we'll decide before we take them home."

Home. I couldn't wait to get all three of them into the amazing nursery we had set up. I couldn't wait to spend my days rocking them to sleep. I couldn't wait to curl up next to my husband and snuggle with the babies beside us.

Life was perfect.

CHAPTER 19
KADE

The last few months had been exhausting. Since bringing the girls home, we'd been going nonstop like the Energizer bunny. There was three of everything. Three diaper changes. Three bottles or rounds of breastfeeding if Lacey could do it. She was on a revolving schedule of pumping her breasts since she couldn't feed all three girls back to back. So she had some breast milk ready for the two who lost out on feeding directly from her. She would switch up, making sure each of the girls got a chance to feed from her. We had three baths, three loads of laundry, and the list went on.

To say we were worn out was an understatement. We barely had time to sleep, relax, or even eat half the time.

Kody had taken my spot as manager at The Cave for a few months because I wanted to stay home and help Lacey. As far as baseball was concerned, Lacey wasn't ready to return yet. However, Tara had informed her that the Sea Dogs had drafted a contract for her to sign for next season. Even if she wanted to play, it would be hard considering she was breastfeeding, and with only two months left in the season, it didn't make sense for her to return to the team.

Despite that, I'd thought Lacey would be more driven to get back to the team and playing, but giving birth seemed to have put things in perspective according to my wife.

"I do want to play again, but you and the girls come first," she'd said after we had had a long and in-depth conversation about her career. "I know I was worried about whether any team would sign me if I took time off, but family comes first."

And now that the Sea Dogs had a contract waiting for her, she didn't have to worry about her career.

Mom was at the house every day, helping us with cooking, cleaning, and washing clothes. Hell, the whole family seemed to be living with us. Kelton's girl, Lizzie, was there any chance she had. The woman was dying to get married and have kids.

We didn't see Ruby and Kross much, but I hadn't expected to either since they had their hands full with their own girls.

Lacey rubbed her eyes as she came into the nursery. "You look sexy sitting in that rocker with Jazlyn cuddled up to you." She stepped deeper into the yellow-and-pink room, which was big enough to hold six babies if need be. She peeked into Julie's crib and then Jordan's.

We settled on the names before we'd left the hospital four months ago.

"Did you get a good nap?" I asked as I rocked Jazlyn. She was our second born, and we'd decided on the name after watching her in the hospital nursery. She seemed to always have a smile on her face when she was sleeping, so Lacey and I thought the name just fit her.

"I did, but I would sleep better if you were in bed with me." She waggled her eyebrows.

I raked my gaze up and down her gorgeous body. She was wearing a Sea Dogs T-shirt and sleep shorts that showed off her toned legs. Lacey was almost back to her pre-pregnancy shape, except for her tits, which were huge now and would be as long as she kept breastfeeding.

She sashayed her sweet body over to a rocking chair beside me. We had three in the room. "You know, maybe we can go out to dinner next weekend. Your mom and Lizzy offered to take care of the girls. We could get a hotel room for a few hours too."

I eased up and onto my feet, careful not to wake Jazlyn. She'd just fallen asleep before Lacey came in. Once she was in her crib, I tugged Lacey out of her chair. "Come here, baby."

She giggled. "Careful of the boobs. They're painful right now. I'm either going to have to feed the girls or pump."

I chuckled as I glanced down at her tits. I was getting hard thinking about the things I would like to do to my wife that I hadn't been able to do in months.

"I'm always gentle," I whispered in her ear before planting my lips on hers.

She moaned, pushing her hips into my groin as our tongues touched for the first time in forever. "Mr. Steel is ready."

"He's been ready," I teased. Actually, I wasn't teasing. My balls were blue.

She flattened her hands on my bare chest. "I think it's time for you to get three more hearts tattooed on your chest."

"I was thinking that very thing yesterday." I wanted to have three small hearts surrounding the one I had with Lacey's name on it.

She dragged her nails down my abs.

I snaked my arms around her waist until I was grabbing her ass and pressing her into me so hard, I let out a groan.

As if the girls knew what we were doing, one of them started crying.

Lacey and I both sagged against each other, huffing out a breath.

So much for an intimate moment or making love to my gorgeous wife.

"I got her," Lacey said as she found Julie crying. "After they're fed, we can pick up where we left off."

"I'm going to take a cold shower." I wasn't kidding.

She giggled. "We'll have our time."

My bare feet sank into the plush carpet as I checked on Jordan and Jazlyn, who were sleeping soundly. Then I kissed Lacey on the neck before she settled in one of the rockers. "I know we will. We have a lifetime together. I couldn't ask for anything more."

And I couldn't. I had a beautiful wife, three adorable girls, a home that was big enough to have more kids, and years upon years to make love and plenty of memories.

The end

MORE MAXWELLS

Would you like to read more about the Maxwell Family? Start the brand new series featuring the Maxwell cousins.

My Heart to Keep - Book 1

The shy ones are diamonds in the rough.

QUINN THOMPSON

When I walk into a room, the popular kids whisper about me. I don't own designer clothes or name-brand shoes. I don't wear low-cut shirts or tons of makeup either. I'm as plain Jane as a girl can get. I live on a farm, where the uniform of the day is boots, jeans, and a T-shirt unless it's winter; then I trade my T-shirts for heavy sweaters and a parka. Baggy is my style.

But I'm considered one of the nerds in school for reasons besides my wardrobe. I have my nose in books while the popular girls have their noses up jocks' butts. I do everything I can to avoid the in crowd at Kensington High—until a new boy waltzes in. He's tall like my brothers, handsome like Zac Efron, and disrupts my belief that boys only want one thing. My only problem is he'll never notice me, not if my arch-nemesis has any say.

MORE MAXWELLS

MAIKEN MAXWELL

Basketball has been my life until my dad died. I'm trying not to get depressed, but it's hard to breathe sometimes. He'll never cheer from the stands at any of my basketball games or shout at me to shoot that three-pointer. I promised him I would step up if anything happened to him, and now it's time to be the man of the house.

Only I'm torn between playing for the Kensington High basketball team and finding a job--until the girl with butterscotch hair snags my attention. She's pretty, quirky, and her presence takes my mind off my troubles. Above all else, she makes me feel things that I've never felt before. In my mind, girls are just a distraction. They're nice to look at, they talk too much, and they're extremely pushy. Yet Quinn Thompson might change my opinion that all girls are created equal.

My Heart to Touch - Book 1
My Heart to Hold - Book 2
My Heart to Give - Book 3
My Heart to Keep - Book 4*

*Coming in 2020

S.B. ALEXANDER

Bestselling author **S.B. Alexander** writes young adult and new adult romances that span the sub-categories of coming of age, sports, paranormal, suspense, and military fiction. Her writing is emotional, angsty, and character driven. She's best known for The Maxwell and The Maxwell Family Saga series.

S.B. or Susan as she likes to be called is a navy veteran, former high school teacher, and former corporate sales executive. She's a lover of sports, especially baseball, although nowadays you can find her glued to the TV during football season.

When she's not writing, she's a full-time caregiver to her soul mate of twenty-one years who got a bad deal in life when he was diagnosed with ALS. Her motto: "Life is too short to waste. So live every moment like it's your last."

You can connect with S.B. Alexander in the following ways:

- facebook.com/sbalexander.authorpage
- twitter.com/sbalex_author
- instagram.com/sbalexanderauthor
- amazon.com/author/sbalexander
- bookbub.com/authors/s-b-alexander

ALSO BY S.B. ALEXANDER

THE MAXWELL SERIES

Upper Young Adult/New Adult Contemporary Romance

Dare to Kiss

Dare to Dream

Dare to Love

Dare to Dance

Dare to Live

Dare to Breathe

The Maxwell Series Boxed Set 1

The Maxwell Series Boxed Set 2

Dare to Kiss Coloring Book Companion

Dare to Embrace^

THE MAXWELL FAMILY SAGA SERIES

Young Adult Contemporary Romance

My Heart to Touch

My Heart to Hold

My Heart to Give

My Heart to Keep*

STANDALONES

New Adult Contemporary Romance

Unforgettable

Breaking Rules

Rescuing Riley

Holding On To Forever

THE HART SERIES

New Adult Romantic Suspense

Hart of Darkness

Hart of Vengeance*

Hart of Redemption*

THE VAMPIRE SEAL SERIES

Young Adult Paranormal Romance

On the Edge of Humanity

On the Edge of Eternity

On the Edge of Destiny

On the Edge of Misery

On the Edge of Infinity

The Vampire SEAL Collection

^Releasing 2019

*Coming 2020.

Visit http://sbalexander.com for all future release dates. Please note release dates are subject to change based on reader demand and the author's schedule. Subscribing to the author's newsletter or following her on Facebook is the best way to stay updated with planned new releases.

www.ingramcontent.com/pod-product-compliance
Lightning Source LLC
Chambersburg PA
CBHW060459080526
44584CB00015B/1476